"I've spent many years, and tens of thousands of dollars, learning the same skills you've easily described in a couple hundred entertaining pages. You have woven the multiple levels of learning into each of the character's lives, even including parenting lessons. Not a single page is wasted. I cannot wait to buy a copy for my entire leadership team. You've easily brought to life a treasure trove of brilliant theory that should be required reading for any leader; community, business, or family. I've read many leadership/management books and I think what you've written is really superior."

> Steve Anderson
> CEO, Legacy

"This book has captured the spirit of leadership in a unique fictional manner allowing readers to experience the lessons of leadership through a compelling story without getting all the scars. I got the concepts and they can be applied day one after reading the book. The story is compelling and drew me in. I found myself wanting to know what was going to happen next. All the characters are spot on and great representations of leaders. This book is almost more realistic and certainly more entertaining than a traditional case study."

> Peter Karlson
> CEO, NeuEon

"I loved this book. It was an easy read and helped me prepare for a difficult meeting I was to facilitate. It is excellent and will become required reading for the GISC coaching program (CDPCC). I loved the story, the characters, and the way you made the story flow. I particularly like the way you repeated the concepts in different ways by the different characters—that made it stick. Can't wait until we can buy it."

> Mary Anne Walk, MS, MBA, MCC
> Executive Director, Gestalt International Study Center

"A must read for managers, leaders, and coaches to learn powerful concepts in an engaging format."

> Sonia March Nevis, PhD
> Co-founder, Gestalt International Study Center

"In this highly engaging and practical book, Nancy Hardaway seamlessly weaves Gestalt leadership principles into a fictionalized account of a dilemma that feels all too real. We are able to relate to each of them as they struggle with their values around power, hierarchy, leadership and their relationships in order to reach a decision that will have a lasting impact on the city that they live in and love. What I found so compelling about this book is that I was drawn into the drama of the story and the personalities of the leaders while learning about leading."

> Joseph Melnick, PhD
> Organizational Consultant
> Co-editor of Mending the World

"I found the book an absorbing story of leadership techniques at once practical and uplifting. If the work of leaders today is increasingly about building relationships and capacitating others, making sense and using teams to derive solutions, this story is an illustrative 'how-to' narrative told through the vehicle of pleasant and supporting fiction."

> Les Schwab, MD
> Chief Medical Director
> Harvard-Vanguard Medical Associates

"It's all here…and very accessible as both a 'primer' with illustrations for someone new to this thinking, and a sophisticated interweaving of how making small shifts in one part of your life has the power to impact the quality of other parts of life. For me, the book perfectly illustrates how rich, dense and deceivingly simple this practice is and I feel a new gratitude for being exposed to it."

> Bev Ryle
> Author of Ground of Your Own Choosing

"I enjoyed this book on so many levels!! I look forward to having a reference copy in my library. You created a story that many types of leaders will relate to and scenarios where many readers will be able to place themselves in the shoes of both the leader and the others. The story is interesting on both a personal level and a professional level, demonstrating and modeling the intertwining of both. It's a *terrific job of creating a story that helps readers see themselves in these challenging situations, without judgment or harsh criticism, heightening their awareness of how these things can happen. You then offered clear and easily digestible thoughts on how to handle difficult situations in a different way than they may have in the past. The story and the way you told it made the lessons come to life and helped the reader understand more about her/himself as a leader in challenging situations and provided what I believe will be seen as new perspectives and new ways to handle familiar old difficulties that could offer more favorable results. Bravo!"*

Jennifer Gould
Sales Consultant
Certified Coach

"I was hooked after the first few pages!! The book is enlightening and different. I have read so many leadership books, many academic and many best sellers. Your approach is so unique and so very helpful. I am actually going to reread it as the learnings are so important but are imparted in such a different way. I'm used to scholarly, academic texts, but this was better because I felt a much more powerful impact. Thank you for sharing your work with me."

Susan J. Ventura, RN, MS
Tobey Hospital, Site Administrator
Associate Chief Nursing Officer, Southcoast Healthcare

"I need to let you know that your book is terrific. Once I allowed myself the time I couldn't put it down. I feel pretty entrenched in this theory and I still learned a great deal."

Robert Ross, EdD
Senior Director, BioTeach Programs
Massachusetts Biotechnology Education Foundation

The
Awareness
Paradigm

A Story of Leadership Success

Nancy Hardaway

Library of Congress Control Number: 2013944470

Nancy Hardaway
The Awareness Paradigm:
A Story of Leadership Success

ISBN 978-1-939166-19-7

A Merrimack Media edition

TABLE OF CONTENTS

Contents

Contents

PREFACE

I work with leaders in industries as varied as banking and fishing; from human services to export services. Their organizations are located from Alaska to Africa, and from New England to the British Isles. I've written this book for them.

In every case, they know their business. It's not the technical expertise they struggle with; it's what they call "the messy people problems:" how to motivate or inspire, how to lead change, how to manage conflict, how to set clear expectations and hold people accountable, how to develop potential. As leaders progress in an organization, their success resides in their ability to get things done through other people.

Those who lead skillfully take us to new places. They see connections between seemingly disparate ideas and issues. They can move easily between detail and broad vision. They inspire us to be better and to do better. They know and share who they are. They help us make things happen and feel good about it.

When I first had the title of leader, I was a twenty-something entrepreneur, with degrees from Tufts and Harvard. I had employees more than twice my age, and though I wasn't quite so arrogant as to think I knew everything, it never occurred to me I had something to learn about leadership.

When you focus only on results and ignore the people, you may get work done but it can be painful and ultimately less effective. I think of a friend who worked on a fascinating project as part of a "Dream Team" of hand picked talents at a high tech firm. The project got done but only three of the many team members were left intact—the others left the company or left their marriages. That's too much collateral damage and organizational loss.

It wasn't until many years later I discovered I could actually learn how to become a better leader. Now I know leadership to be a way of seeing, and a set of skills that can be taught and learned, just like I can learn how to play golf, play piano, or speak Italian. It's not just a role or a title, and it isn't in your DNA. Some may have more natural talent than I, but if I'm willing to learn and practice I can get a lot better at it, and I can be a leader from any seat in the house.

In those intervening years I founded and sold two companies, won national sales awards and served as editor of a business magazine, was a banker and a CEO of an international organization. Sometimes I led from a position of power, and sometimes I led from the front lines. I found my way over those years through trial and error—not a particularly rapid or effective way to learn.

I finally started reading the literature of the time on leadership. Warren Bennis and Peter Senge. Books like *Good to Great. The One Minute Manager. Who Moved My Cheese. Fish Tales.* I even brought in the team behind the "Fish" books to teach my whole company.

I discovered some great ideas. Sadly, I forgot most of them in the midst of day-to-day pressures. It wasn't until I found my way to the model of leadership I present here, a way of looking at myself and the world and human behavior as an integrated system and learning to practice a more effective way of interacting in that system, that I started to actually *become* a better leader.

Now I spend all my time helping others find the best in themselves and their people through my company, Listening 2 Leaders. To satisfy clients who wanted a way to share their leadership learning and kept asking for something to hand their employees, I put pen to paper (or fingers to keyboard).

In preparing to write, I deconstructed my own leadership process and development. I tracked the challenges my clients share with me. I made lists of the abilities and skills I wanted to present for readers. I reviewed materials from leadership training I've developed and programs in leadership and coaching I have both taken and taught. I interviewed and observed other leaders. I kept coming back to this quote from a friend and colleague:

"The most important thing for a leader is the dual process function, at the same time being able to pay attention to content and process."

- John Wipfler, MBA, JD, CEO

In order to manage, you need to have a highly sensitized and flexible awareness "palate." You need to be able to pick up on subtle nuances that require focused attention, and on broader winds of change that require wide-angle sensing and seeing. You need to know who you are and how you impact others.

I wanted to write a book that would enhance this macro-skill. A traditional how-to book of theory and lessons wasn't coming alive. The real learning for participants in training comes from experiential exercises, not listening to theory. Likewise in coaching, we focus on development goals through whatever challenges come up in ongoing daily work.

I knew the reader would learn best by experiencing the leadership journey directly. The lessons would be more accessible in fiction form, immediately applicable and resonant over time. Leadership happens through people, and readers need to see the story of real leaders interacting on these pages. The result is the story of Cesar, Redley, Fletcher, Mark, and Julia.

I end in praise of support. Too often, as leaders, we try to go it alone, to demonstrate our strength and independence. I've had to learn to ask for and be willing to receive support from others.

Thanks to the many who improvised roles, read early drafts, read later drafts, and gave needed feedback, particularly my son Trevor Harrison, friend and colleague Laurie Fitzpatrick, and my book group Pam Burke, Adriana Sheedy, and Marty Zurn (The Divas). Thanks also to my daughter, Dr. Krista Harrison, who was finishing her dissertation in Bioethics at Johns Hopkins and had no time to read my chapters but offered lots of moral support. Thanks to Rick Mauer for his ideas on resistance and tips on marketing. Thanks to my editor, Jennifer Powell, and my publisher, Jenny Hudson.

Special thanks to Karen Geary of DK Geary Brewing Company in Portland, Maine, for a private brewery tour and detailed explanations of the brewing process, and the beer business. Thanks also to Solms Delta winery of Franschhoek, South Africa and to Maine Meadery of Portland, Maine for private mead-making tours and tastings. Most importantly, thanks to my husband, Larry Peterson, for always offering unconditional support for my leadership and writing journey.

I would not have finished this book without the ongoing dedicated support of Dr. Joseph Melnick, business consultant, psychotherapist, senior faculty and director at GISC, and former editor of the Gestalt Review. He read chapters as they emerged from my computer, urged me on when I flagged, discussed theory and characters, and provided great writing process ideas. He has my boundless appreciation. It would be impossible to repay his generosity so I can only try to pass it on to others, and also to wish him a lifetime of high quality dark chocolate.

INTRODUCTION

T he four leaders in the story are entirely fictional but their challenges are real. You'll meet people who will look familiar because they share common struggles and concerns with you and your colleagues. In an easy and entertaining read, you'll learn simple but powerful ways of increasing your own success, immediately applicable to leadership at any level and any type of organization.

Have you ever thought it would be easier to work with others if you just had more power? Meet Cesar Smith, the former police chief turned mayor who says it was easier being a leader when he could carry a gun. He needs to convince a committee of high-powered leaders to work together and make a crucial decision and worries that he's lost his edge along with the millions of dollars at stake. You'll be frustrated right along with Cesar in the first few pages as you watch the committee work hard, but at cross purposes, and identify with a few painful meetings you may have experienced yourself.

Here's your chance to be an outside observer to a group working together. You'll learn how to analyze their behavior and explore what it will take for them to be more effective. You'll experience their interactions changing dramatically with a little outside help, and learn how to create a high-potential team in the process.

The initial failure of the team is not due to their lack of technical knowledge or experience, but they each bring their unique leadership challenges to the table. You'll meet the successful banker who's analytical and risk-averse, good at numbers but less effective with his staff and his family.

Then there's the smart, caring doctor. Over the years he's created a very successful medical practice and urgent clinic but can't figure out why his team is so resistant to a major change initiative or how to get them to buy in.

The founder of a brewery and meadery runs one of the few growing businesses in town. Though passionate about her product and her people, her leadership style may be getting in the way of her success and satisfaction.

Though there's not a perfect ending for everyone, they all learn something along the way through their work with the consultant, Julia Breuer. Watch her carefully because mentoring and developing your people is one of a leader's most important roles. You'll see Julia help them learn new skills and find answers they didn't know they had.

As you read the story and get to know the characters, you'll learn how to put those ideas of leadership success to work in your own world. The chapters are short and present one idea at a time to provide an easy way to take in new information (in spite of all that is exalted by multi-tasking achievers).

Once you've enjoyed the story, you can continue to enhance your skills of how to make things happen in the world. Appendix A lists each chapter's main idea along with a snippet of the action to provide an easy way for you to find and reread or discuss the individual lessons in the book with colleagues or with your team. Appendix B is a resource for those who want a bit more theory.

PROLOGUE

The mid-winter morning still felt more night than day. Yesterday's snow had turned into a cold drizzle. The clouds obscured the mountains surrounding the town. It would have been a good day to roll over and go back to sleep. Mayor Cesar Smith didn't have that luxury.

It was still dark as he drove from his home in the foothills into town. He couldn't even see the harbor. Just for luck, he took a left and passed the big old mill building decaying along the river. Its many tall windows were shuttered in plywood. The piles of trash and weeds that had collected around the foundation were coated in thinning layers of dirty snow. Graffiti grew increasingly bold across the brick walls.

As bad as it looked, Cesar could see its promise. The community leaders on his committee did too. He knew if they could get the multi-million dollar grant, this building would be the catalyst for a turnaround of the town's decline. He had based his election on the potential of this grant. Unfortunately, each leader had a totally different idea of what would be the best use, and the grant required a unanimous vote. He groaned as he thought about their progress and the fast approaching deadline. The harder he tried to get them to agree, the more their once tentative individual ideas had hardened into battle lines.

"This morning will be different," Cesar assured himself, as he turned onto Main Street and pulled into his spot in the town hall parking lot. He walked briskly to the conference room, optimistic that his amicable lunches with the committee members over the past few days would turn things around.

He started last Monday at the yacht club with Fletcher Harrington, president of the regional bank. Fletcher would bring the local funding required by the grant. Though the town's fortunes had faded, the bank had tripled in size through acquisitions around the region.

Tuesday, Cesar met Dr. Mark Green at the diner across from his clinic and urgent care center. As owner and medical director, Mark never had much free time, but he had a deep passion for the town and the people that lived in it. If not for Mark, people would have to drive a long way for their healthcare.

For the final meeting on Thursday, Cesar took Redley Wilson to a local pub that served the beer she produced in her fast growing brewery, the town's sole successful local business story. Redley had the entrepreneur's perspective along with the energy and the optimism of youth that they all needed.

By 8:30 it was clear to Cesar that the lunches hadn't done a darn thing. The dregs of coffee were cold on the table, and Cesar's pock-marked skin was turning bright red as he watched his Blue Ribbon Committee yelling at each other. Even Mark, who usually liked to be the peacemaker, was being just as stubborn as the other two.

"That's it! I've had it!" said Cesar. "I'm not letting these millions slip away because you all can't make a decision together. I'll disband this committee and choose three other leaders. Real leaders."

"But Mayor..." they said, almost in unison, in agreement for the first time in months.

Their first meetings back before Christmas had been so polite. They were energized as they brainstormed lots of different ideas for the building. Then, somehow, they'd each focused on a different "highest and best use." A month ago, Cesar had taken them on a trip to tour a successful grant winner in another state, hoping that seeing the difference it had made for that town would give them a common perspective. But they'd argued the whole four-hour return trip, as if they'd each seen a completely different building. And here they were at it again.

Cesar didn't let any of them speak. "What choice are you giving me? I've never had a team like this. You call yourselves leaders? How do you get anything done in your own businesses?"

"This is completely different! I call the shots at my bank. I don't have to listen to them." Fletcher turned angrily to the others at the table. "This is not *my* fault!" He pushed his chair away from the table and stood up, tightening the knot on the club tie that he had loosened earlier. He reached behind him and picked up his black wool overcoat.

"Sit down, Fletcher. You're as much at fault as the others," said Cesar.

"That's for sure," said Redley, her red hair almost electric with her fury as she jumped to her feet. In her high-heeled boots she was nose to nose with Fletcher. "I call the shots at my brewery, too, you know. And it's growing a lot faster than your bank! You're so pig-headed with your old-fashioned opinions. Get him off the committee, Mayor, and we'll all do better." She sat back down and looked at Mark. "Right Doc?"

"Calm down, both of you," said Mark, rubbing his salt and pepper goatee with irritation. "Frankly, at this point I'd be okay with you replacing me, Mayor. I've got problems at my clinic to solve. I don't have time for any more road trips or anything."

"Forget it, Mark," said the mayor. "You're not getting out of this that easy." Perspiration beaded up on his forehead.

The mayor looked around the conference room table at his team, his dark bushy eyebrows almost a single line across his forehead. He took a deep breath, held it, then blew it out forcefully. "I thought I'd picked the right leaders when I picked you. Frankly, I still do." He stopped and was quiet for a moment, then nodded. "We'll just have to meet more often so we make the grant deadline in May."

He looked from face to face, his dark eyes daring them to challenge him. No one said a word. "And I'll call in outside help to work with us. A consultant who can get to a solution for that building. For our whole town."

"Mayor," said Fletcher, looking over his glasses. "No consultant will know as much as the four of us. Plus, you know there's no money in the budget for that."

"I'll find some way to get you three to make a decision, even if I have to pay for it myself! Anyway, they voted funds at town meeting for experts to help us with this project."

"Experts?" burst out Fletcher. "That money was for engineers and architects and land planners. We're the experts on our town!"

"Enough! I'll do what I have to. Just plan your schedules so you can meet twice a week from now on." There was something different in his tone that got their attention. He closed his thick, dog-eared folder decisively and hoisted himself from his chair.

"Meeting adjourned," he said.

The bluster of his anger deflated quickly so by the time he approached his office his broad shoulders drooped in defeat. He squared them up before passing his assistant. With that one move, even in a blue blazer, white shirt, and khaki pants he looked more tough cop than mayor.

He crossed the threadbare carpet and sat down at his desk. He picked up the phone and punched in some numbers. His wife answered on the first ring.

"Call your mother," he said. "Get the phone number of that consultant she suggested. Might help me with this damn team."

"I already have it," said his wife. "She gave it to me last week after you described the situation. Hang on." After a long pause, she read off a number. "Cesar, I know how you hate to ask for help. Good for you for calling someone."

He sat slumped in his chair for a long time, fingering the paper he'd written the number on. Finally he took a deep breath and dialed. Little did he know that the call would not only be the answer he was looking for, but would also be the beginning of a whole new way of approaching leadership for him and all three members of the committee.

"Julia Breuer," said the clear, crisp voice answering the phone.

He told her he'd been referred by his mother-in-law. "I don't know much about consultants but she's one tough cookie so I figured she'd find me someone good. She deals with warring factions all the time."

"I suppose that's one way to describe labor negotiations," agreed Julia. "You're having a labor union issue?"

"No. Worse. It's a project team of damn stubborn leaders. We've got a deadline and we're not making any progress."

"So what's going on?" asked Julia.

The mayor described the mill building rehab opportunity, the grant, and the three members of his hand-picked committee.

"I've got a conservative bank president who is all about the numbers. A kind of Hippie small business owner—very creative, full of ideas. And a doctor. His focus is really people. Nice guy. And me? I guess I just want results. They're all so good at what they do, I assumed this would be easy. Wrong!"

Julia laughed. "Bringing leaders or experts to work together is nearly always challenging."

"That's for sure." The mayor flipped open the folder in front of him, then closed it again. "I don't know what else to tell you."

"Mayor," said Julia gently, "you've described your situation, but not what you need. How would you like me to help you?"

He sighed and closed his eyes as he slumped back in his chair. "I don't know. Frankly, I'm not even sure you can. Maybe I just need to start over with a new team."

"You want help with assembling a new group?"

He was quiet for a minute. "No!" He sat up decisively. "No. I don't want to backtrack. I've only got three months to get to a unanimous decision and then convince the town it's the right one. Besides, I've already got the right people for the job."

"So you want me to help you and your team reach a decision together?"

"Yes, exactly. Will you analyze all their proposals and tell us what to do?" he asked.

"That's not how I work," said Julia. "You all know more than I could possibly know about the issues you're working on."

"Fletcher would like that comment," observed the mayor thoughtfully. "But they don't even listen to each other anymore. The longer we go on, the more stuck we get."

"That can happen."

"So maybe that's it. I need help getting them to listen to each other again. And agree on something," said Cesar, with more energy. "Can you do that?"

"Ahhh. That I can help you with," said Julia.

The mayor's shoulders visibly relaxed. "How?"

"I help you figure out what you're doing—both you as the leader and the team as a whole. Then I help you build on your strengths to work more effectively," she explained.

Cesar frowned. "Yeah, strengths, okay. Then you have to figure out what's wrong, don't you? And tell us what to change?"

"I don't look at it quite that way. I do help you get out of the trenches and get a new perspective. Starting with what's working rather than giving you a list of what's not working is faster and more effective."

"I like faster. That's exactly what I need," said Cesar. "According to my mother-in-law you get results. When can you come in?"

‵‵‵‵‵‵‵‵‵

Redley walked into her office and threw her purple briefcase on her desk in disgust. Her assistant appeared at the doorway as she hung up her coat on the coat rack in the corner.

"What's up?" he asked.

"The Blue Ribbon Committee," she said, flipping through a pile of mail on the desk.

"Still no progress?"

"No, and now the mayor is going to have us meet more often. Like I have time for that. I was here until ten last night as it was. He wants to bring in a consultant. I think I can help him find someone he could use, though."

"Do you have just a couple minutes to help me first?"

She dropped the mail and looked up. Her assistant described the challenge he was having consolidating ideas on the new customer management software. Redley examined the lists he handed her, then quickly pulled out a pad and started writing. She ripped off the page and gave it to him.

"There you go. That should do it. Now find that guy that did the strategic planning with the bottling supplier. He'd be a good consultant to help the mayor."

"I'll get on it," he said as he turned to leave. "Thanks for the help. Listen, Margo needs help in shipping when you get a chance. Oh, and your husband called about an hour ago."

Redley sighed. The meeting had gone so long she'd missed their coffee date, and tomorrow he'd be back out of town on another cross-country flight.

She used her cell phone's speed dial to call him. As she waited, she opened her computer.

Her office was in the left wing of an old theater she'd reclaimed on the edge of town. If she looked out her window she could see the river rushing over rocks on its way to the bay, and the once grand houses lining its banks on the far side, but she rarely noticed.

"Blast!" she said, hanging up after leaving a message for her husband. She started working on an overdue proposal.

"Boss Lady," said the young man in knee high rubber boots at her doorway. "I got a problem with one of the new tanks."

"I'm coming," she said. She pulled off her dress boots and slipped into the bright red rubber boots that were always nearby.

As she followed him, she tried to force down the anxiety of an overwhelming list of urgent to-do's. Interruptions inevitably meant long days, but hands-on leadership was what had always worked for her, what had enabled her to get out from under her start-up debt. She had vowed in those early days she'd never borrow from a family member again and so far she'd kept that promise.

`````````
`````````

Fletcher strode into the bank and took the elevator up eight floors to his office suite. The whole top of the building was lined with glass walled offices for the bank's executive team. Although people looked up, he walked to his corner office without greeting anyone. They were used to it. His secretary was waiting with coffee for him and a list of phone messages and appointments. He took the coffee, motioning for her to follow.

She handed him the messages and started reading off appointments once he hung up his suit jacket and sat down.

He interrupted her. "What's wrong with the mayor, Angie?" He didn't wait for an answer. "He's a Democrat. Doesn't see the value of time and money, that's what."

"Yes, I know," said Angie carefully. "Listen, Mr. Harrington, can we…"

"I'm tired of this committee. I can't understand why the mayor and I couldn't have just made the decision ourselves and called it unanimous. After all, the bank's going to be involved. I'm bringing the local money. He's bringing the grant funding. That should be it, right?"

Angie nodded.

"I say this every week, don't I?" Fletcher asked.

Angie nodded again. "So…"

"Well, now you'll hear it twice a week. You'll have to move some things around on my calendar, I know, but I can't let them meet without me. Who knows what decisions they'd make? The worst of it is now he wants to bring in some outside consultant. Why he thinks we need to spend money on a consultant is beyond me. What can an outsider tell us we don't already know? I've been in this town for thirty years. A lot longer than the mayor, right?"

"Yes," said Angie. "He came that year of the bad floods, remember?"

"Don't mention that year. That was the just the beginning of the decline here. He'll learn the hard way that consultants are a waste of time."

"Listen," said Angie, her voice a bit rushed. "Can we talk for a minute?"

He shook his head as looked at his watch. "I can't, because…"

The phone on his desk rang. Angie crossed the room and answered it. "Mr. Harrington's office…. He's not available…. Oh, yes. He's right here." She handed him the phone.

He turned red as he listened briefly then slammed the phone down. "It's the high school. I've got to go. They want me to pick up my son. Right now. He was suspended."

〰〰〰〰〰

Mark drove to his office with the windows half open, both for his shaggy dog Muldoon, and himself. The dog liked the wind blowing his ears back and the damp cold air helped clear Mark's thoughts. Wrangling at these meetings always gave him a headache.

He parked his Range Rover in the back lot, waited for Muldoon to finish his business, then walked into the clinic. One of the docs was in the back hallway and Muldoon leaped up to greet him, almost spilling the coffee cup he was carrying. "Down," yelled Mark repeatedly, all the while apologizing. Finally he had to grab the dog by the collar and almost drag him into the storeroom that was Muldoon's personal clinic home.

"Sorry about that," said Mark. "He gets so excited with people in white coats."

"I don't know why you always bring him in, then," muttered the other doc, brushing the dirt off his lapels with his free hand.

"You know there's no one to let him out at home," answered Mark as he headed into the kitchen.

"If you're looking for coffee I finished it. You just getting in? We need to talk."

Mark opened the cabinet, starting to make more coffee. "I had a meeting of that town committee I'm on. There's something to finally be hopeful about. The mayor's calling in an expert to help us."

"That's great. Listen, I need some help too. That's what I need to talk about. I keep telling you I can't keep up to date with all my patient electronic records. The new system takes too long. You'll have to find another way, okay?"

Mark tried to convince his colleague to give it more time, but the other doctor wasn't buying it. In the end Mark gave up. He agreed to arrange for one of the office staff to finish the records each day. "Just for now, okay? You'll have to learn it sometime," he said in frustration to the back of the departing white coat. "And don't tell anyone else."

Chapter 1

"You're not quite what I expected," Mayor Cesar Smith said, as he met Julia in his office. She was tiny, even in high heels.

"Is that good or bad?" she asked with a laugh, looking up at him with a steady open gaze. Although her shoulder length hair was white, her face was young. She was elegantly dressed, with a bright blue silk scarf draped around her shoulders. She shook his hand firmly.

"I'm not sure," he said, more to himself than to her. "Maybe I should have hired a referee, or a bouncer."

"Maybe you just did," she said grinning. "Let's sit a minute." She gestured to the round table by the tall windows of his office overlooking empty storefronts. He followed hurriedly, pulling out a chair for her.

"I'm counting on you to get this group past their differences to agree," he said, sitting down heavily in one of the chairs, barely big enough for his girth. "What the hell is wrong with them?"

"Differences are great because you get lots of ideas, lots of energy," said Julia.

"Oh yeah, there's certainly energy. Energy to yell at each other."

"Well, that's the downside." She shrugged. "Our differences make working together harder."

"You know, I used to be the Chief of Police in this town and I had no problems. At least no problems with my teams. After I retired, I thought I could still help this town so I ran for mayor. Maybe I've lost my edge. Or maybe I just don't have the right personality for this kind of job."

"It's unlikely to be your edge or your personality. Just new leadership challenges."

"Feels more like failure. I'm just not sure if it's theirs or mine."

"Listen. I know you're a good leader, Mayor. I've read about you. You're just facing a new situation—it's not leading by title or top down anymore."

"It was easier when I wore a gun." He patted his hip pocket.

She chuckled and nodded. "But a lot of leadership is about influence, not power, right?"

"Speaking of which," Cesar said, looking at his watch, "I'm sorry I can't do more than bring you over and introduce you right now. This budget hearing is too important for me to miss, with finances being so tough. Fletcher Harrington is leading the meeting until I can get there. Will you be okay or should we wait until next week to get you involved?"

She grinned. There was a little mischief in her expression.

"I'll be just fine," she assured him.

Walking down the hall, they heard the strident voices in the conference room from a distance. The mayor looked down at the tiny woman walking calmly beside him, her heels on the worn marble floor a staccato punctuation to her steps.

"They're at it again, obviously," he said, frowning.

"Lot of energy in the room and it's so early," she said. "That's a good sign."

"Hmmph," he responded doubtfully.

As the mayor opened the door and allowed Julia to enter the room, the voices quieted and silence surrounded them. The three committee members looked up and then at each other. Cesar rushed to introduce Julia, spending a bit too long on her credentials, as if he felt she needed extra credibility.

"Team expert, highly successful business owner, former music teacher, former sports coach, top notch business consultant, and best in the business to help us," he summed up. "I'll be back as soon as I can." He hurried back out into the hall, closing the door behind him.

"Please," said Julia, as she settled gracefully into a chair against the wall. "You're in the middle of something. Go on. I'll just watch quietly for now."

Fletcher didn't need any more invitation than that. "That will be just fine." He turned to the other two, looking over the top of his glasses. "I have a report here from my marketing department on the survey they completed of some of our customers who live in town. But I'd like to move on to the data from the engineers." He started reading statistics aloud from a thick folder.

"This evidence proves it conclusively," he said with a small smile. "The building footprint will not have to be enlarged and the parking will be more than sufficient for my cultural center, so therefore…"

"Don't pontificate for the audience, Fletch," interrupted Redley, pushing her thick bangs off her face. "We've heard this before. I've said it before and I'll say it again. Your symphony hall will bring in old people for a concert here and there. Fine. But most of the time the building will be empty. We already have an empty Main Street! That can't be the highest and best use that the grant requires."

"It's a cultural center. Culture! Are you familiar with culture? It's not just for old people. It's for the whole town. Education programs for kids, afternoons and weekends…"

"But it's not maximizing the potential of the place! Of all people, you should get that, being a banker. You understand economics. Using that building for a business incubator is perfect. Young creative people love funky reclaimed space. There's square footage enough for offices and a lobby area or courtyard type of thing to collaborate. They'll use it day and night…"

"Great, just what we need," Fletcher interrupted. "Noise problems in the middle of the night. That's ridiculous. The whole idea is ridiculous. A business incubator is not appropriate for that building. It brings in start-ups. People without cash. When they get money, they'll leave! You ought to know that."

"Fletcher, Redley, stop already," said Mark, putting his palms up as if separating a fight. "It's not about money. I keep telling you, this is an amazing building right in the center of town that appears to be big enough for a full athletic complex as well as a community center. We'll never find the square footage elsewhere to…"

Fletcher and Redley started yelling at once. "That's not what we need." "We need young start ups." "The performing arts…" "Healthy exercise…" "businesses with people there all the time…" "acoustic possibilities for the concert hall…"

The yelling continued until Mark finally turned to Julia. "Do something," he pleaded.

Chapter 2

J ulia said something but Mark couldn't even hear her.
"Everyone, wait!" said Mark, standing up. Finally
Fletcher noticed and stopped yelling at Redley.
"What?" he asked Mark.

"We're going over the same ground, Fletcher," said Mark.
"I think we should stop and welcome Julia and see how she
can help."

"We have business to discuss," answered Fletcher without
even glancing at Julia.

"Yes, I know, but I think we need to stop and say hello,"
answered Mark quietly. He swiveled his chair so he was
looking at Julia. "We want to, well… as the required human
services representative, I personally would like to welcome
you. I trust you can help us." He reached his hand out toward
her and nodded.

"I'm sure I can," said Julia as she shook his hand. "I look
forward to getting to know you better."

"Me, too," said Redley, "although I'm surprised the
mayor found a consultant so fast. I was going to help him
find someone, but I'm glad I don't have to now. I'm the
small business rep on the committee—anointed because I
complained too much in town meeting." She laughed. "And
that's the truth."

"I'm the financial expert," said Fletcher, shuffling his
papers on the table. "Now then, let's get back to work. The
mayor is holding me accountable for our progress…"

"What progress, Fletch?" said Redley. "Maybe we'll actually
make some progress if we can get Julia's help."

"I think we do need help, Fletcher," said Mark quietly.

Julia turned to Fletcher with a questioning look. "May I
share something I noticed?"

"You aren't really asking for my permission," he said, "since
you'll go ahead anyway."

She shook her head. "I won't. Actually, it's a real question. This is your meeting, so I am asking for your permission."

Fletcher stopped. He turned fully to face Julia, looking both surprised and curious.

"Thank you for that, at least." He closed his folder. "All right, fine. I don't know how you can help, but fine. Take over," he said, gesturing for her to move to the head of the table.

Julia put up her hands. "I don't run your meetings. That's not my role."

"Then what?" asked Fletcher. "How do you propose to help us?"

"I help you pay closer attention to how you work together. Not just the content but the patterns of the way you work that help you... and that sometimes cause you to get stuck. Like now."

"That makes no sense," retorted Fletcher. "The only patterns we need to look at are on these documents here. Then we need to make a decision."

"Just let her explain, Fletcher," implored Mark.

Fletcher glanced at his watch but then gestured for Julia to continue.

"As Fletcher said, you need to produce a decision," agreed Julia. "So how do you get there? Making a decision in a group is complicated. It takes some complex interactions. I look at the 'How' of the decision, not the 'What.'"

"So process versus product?" asked Redley. "I get that, being sort of in the manufacturing business."

"I don't," said Mark.

"You know," Redley said, turning to Mark. "My products are beer and mead. The process is how I go about making each one. From the ingredients, to how I move it through the different pieces of equipment and so forth. I'm always tweaking the process to save money, time, and to make a better product."

"Exactly," agreed Julia. "I look at the ingredients of how you work together. How Fletcher, or the mayor, leads you. How you respond. What you focus on. I look for the patterns and opportunities to tweak the process, to use Redley's words. Small changes can make big differences."

The door opened and the mayor entered.

"Is there hope for us?" he asked, looking at Julia. He was somewhat breathless, and he didn't pause for an answer. "I rushed back over here. Based on my last meeting, we need something to change this town's fortunes, that's for damn sure. I hope you've made progress. What do you think, Julia?"

She looked around the table and nodded. "You've chosen your team well, Mayor."

"Fine. So what's wrong?" Cesar settled into the chair at the end of the table opposite Fletcher. "Why can't we reach a single decision?"

"First, may I tell you what I see that's working well?" Julia took a moment to scan the four faces.

Fletcher rolled his eyes. Julia caught his gaze and held it until he nodded just slightly.

"Here's the thing, Mayor," she said. "Teams develop their own work styles."

"And my team?" asked Cesar.

"What I've already noticed is your team's willingness and ability to state their opinions with conviction."

Redley nodded. Mark shrugged. Fletcher took off his glasses and cleaned them.

"We all state our opinions," said Fletcher. "Seems like that's necessary for leaders. What's your point?"

"Great question. It is an important skill you all do easily. I see groups where no one is willing to state their opinion, or if they do they give in as soon as they're challenged."

"Clearly they get nothing done, then," said Fletcher.

"On the contrary. Sometimes they make decisions very quickly because there's no conflict. Someone offers an idea, they all agree and that's the decision. Just not necessarily the best decision."

"But that's not this team," said the mayor, jumping in quickly.

"Correct," said Julia. "You articulate your opinions clearly. You're great at advocating for your point of view. In fact, you're all so committed to stating your opinions with passion, you'll restate them no matter how many times it takes, right?"

"That's the problem," said Mark. "Over and over again."

Julia laughed. "Still, it's important to have energy and commitment to your ideas. It's what's allowed each of you to be so successful in your careers. It will ultimately make you a great team."

"Really?" asked the mayor doubtfully.

Julia nodded emphatically. "When no one disagrees, assumptions don't get challenged. No testing of ideas. No alternatives to choose from. You don't know where each other stands."

Redley grinned. "That's definitely not our problem."

"Right. You have clarity," agreed Julia.

"But it's not getting us anywhere," said the mayor.

"It's a starting point—knowing what you do often, what you do well," said Julia. "Appreciate it and see its value. Then use it as a choice, not a default. See what other behaviors are available that you're not doing. What's missing."

"I remember we started out very polite, taking time to listen," said Mark thoughtfully. "Gradually we've grown… what…. More argumentative. Maybe bolder is the polite term. Yes, bolder and more opinionated."

"Often happens with teams as they form," said Julia. "Back when I was coaching, field hockey season started with players being polite to each other, and attentive to me. After a few weeks, their differences started to play out. I'd hear arguments in the locker room and on the field, and they'd challenge me. I'd see it happen in teams at my companies, too."

"That sounds all too familiar," said the mayor.

"If that's what happened on your teams, my dear lady," said Fletcher, articulating each word carefully, "Clearly, you cannot possibly be of any help to us."

Redley gasped.

Chapter 3

"We'll see, Fletcher," said Julia, slowly. "That's always a slight possibility when teams don't want help."

Cesar frowned as he looked over at Fletcher and twisted the big gold ring on his finger. "Continue, Julia."

"What I'm saying is that your problem is *not* that you state your opinions and disagree, nor should you stop doing it. Your problem is you're stuck in it. You need to find alternative behaviors to add. That's what my teams did."

"So what do we do?" asked Cesar? "Do we need rules?"

Julia smiled. "There are a few rules, or guidelines I've found that help groups to work more successfully together. One would be particularly useful here."

"Great." The mayor pushed himself out of his chair and grabbed the marker sitting on a ledge under the flip chart. He tapped the marker on the pad and smiled, his mustache curling around his lips. "Fine. That's what we need. Rules for success. Give them here and I'll write them down and make sure everyone follows them."

"Just write some big question marks," said Julia.

The mayor wrote four big blue question marks. "Now what?" His marker was poised over the paper.

"That's the important one for now. You are all so good at stating your opinions…"

"Yes, yes, yes," Fletcher interrupted. "Look at the time, Mayor."

"We'll get back to work in just a minute," insisted the mayor. "I like the idea of rules. Julia, give them all to me."

She told the mayor what else to write and he completed the flip chart and sat down.

They all looked at the flip chart:

- ????

- Time Sharing

- Refocusing Your Lens

"I don't see…" started Fletcher. Redley shushed him.

Mark spoke up quickly. "The first one is clearly about asking questions. What about those other two? Time Share? Refocus?"

"From what I've observed so far, you're already good at time sharing," said Julia.

"Real estate ownership?" asked Fletcher.

"You may be sarcastic, Mr. Harrington, but there actually is a similarity," responded Julia quickly. "Time share in real estate is fractional ownership, right?"

Fletcher grudgingly agreed. "Share of time, share of responsibility for cost."

"Sharing available time and responsibility matters on a team, too," said Julia. "In my field hockey example, it's not hogging the ball or hanging back too far out of the action, letting the others do all the work."

"I think we're good at that," observed Mark. "We all contribute, all speak up."

"What's that last one?" asked Redley. "Refocus your lens? What does that mean?"

"That's the toughest to see from the outside. And toughest to explain," said Julia.

She shared a metaphor of a camera lens that can be shifted from close up focus on detail to wide-angle panoramic view, pointed at another person or turned around and pointed at yourself. Then she compared it to how they focused their attention.

"For a team to be successful you have to be able to shift from the details to the big picture. That's the content. You also shift your attention from the stuff you're talking about to how you're all working together. That's what I'm helping you do now."

"Okay, great. So let's get back to work," said Cesar. "How do teams use these rules?"

"Just pick one at a time to focus on," answered Julia. "Pick the key action that you think will make a difference. Try it. See what happens."

"We're stuck in our own opinions," said Cesar, thinking out loud. "So we stop making statements and ask questions?"

"That's a good question. You want to ask questions, yes, but in addition to, not instead of," she answered. "You absolutely don't want to stop what you do well."

"So we keep... what was your word? Advocating? We keep advocating, right, but we add in questions," said Redley.

"Right," agreed Julia. "Ask real questions of one another. Where you don't already know the answer. Get curious. Then notice whether you get an answer."

"So let's get back to business using Julia's suggestion," said Cesar. "Make sure you ask some questions."

Redley jumped in. "Okay. I'll bite. Fletcher, you said before you did a little survey of some bank customers that live in town. How did it come out?"

Fletcher carefully picked up the papers and flipped through the pile. "It's here on page four." He read out the numbers. "Thirty-four percent for the cultural center, thirty-seven percent for the community gym, and twenty-nine percent for the business building. Unfortunately, it's too small a sample to be statistically significant. If you want them, I can find the actual numbers."

Redley shook her head. They all looked at Julia, except Fletcher who was still looking for the data.

"That question didn't seem to help us much," said Mark, looking at Julia.

"Good start, though," Julia responded. "It's natural that you use questions for getting information, getting data. There are other kinds of questions to ask, though."

"This is ridiculous, Ms. Breuer," said Fletcher. "We don't need a grammar lesson about questions."

"No, and I'm not an English teacher, Mr. Harrington," said Julia sharply.

"Go Julia!" said Redley.

Fletcher turned to glare at Redley. "You sound like my teenage son."

Redley just grinned and shrugged. "So what do you mean?" she asked Julia.

"Curiosity," said Julia. "It's not just the question that matters, it's being willing to put aside your own point of view momentarily to explore theirs. How does it look from where they sit?"

"Why?" asked Fletcher.

"If that's a real question, I'll answer," said Julia. Fletcher nodded grudgingly so she continued. "Helps to expand thinking, reassess your own viewpoint. It opens up the boundaries of the conversation. It can lead to new answers, more creative solutions."

"I've done enough thinking and I believe I already have the right answer," said Fletcher.

"It also helps the others get more interested in you and your perspective," added Julia, "if you're willing to try to look at it from theirs."

Mark jumped in this time. "So I am curious about what you think of the data, Fletcher. Was it what you expected?"

"Ummm. I… No. But it doesn't matter because it's such a small sample."

Redley jumped in again. "I have a different question."

"Wait," said Julia. "Did Mark get an answer?"

"No," said Mark. "At least not completely, so let me ask again, because now I'm even more curious. Why wasn't it what you expected, Fletcher? What did you expect?"

He shrugged. "I assumed they'd be far more in favor of my cultural center. It's an obvious need to me. I don't know why they didn't see that."

Mark nodded. "The results just struck me the same way. I would have assumed they'd have overwhelmingly gone for the community center. Seems obvious."

"Why don't you ask a question, Fletcher," prompted Redley.

"I'm not ready to ask a question," snapped Fletcher.

"Well, I have a question for the mayor, okay?" asked Redley. Fletcher nodded. "Look, you all know I think this building would be great for start ups because they'd create jobs." She turned to the mayor. "Chief, I'm curious what kind of jobs you think are most important to see in our town?"

"New jobs are crucial," Cesar agreed. "We need to create full time professional jobs. With salaries high enough to sustain a family."

"What else?" asked Redley.

"A variety of part-time jobs and internships would be great for our high school and college students and help the retirees that need to subsidize their fixed incomes. Maybe flex time positions for stay-at-home parents."

Everyone sat in silence, looking at the mayor.

Finally Redley tapped one blue painted fingernail on the table gently. "Anything making you curious, Chief?" she asked in a loud whisper.

The mayor shifted in his chair. "Right. Um. Questions. Okay. What about a question for Fletcher. Redley's brought up jobs. What types of jobs do you think your cultural center would create?"

Fletcher flipped to another page in the stack of papers in front of him. "According to the business plan that my team created, the operation of the center would generate ten full-time positions, but then if we did create the symphony, those would be eighty part-time salaries for musicians." Fletcher's voice sounded energized. He suddenly seemed more engaged. "Maybe part-time box office and usher type jobs. The youth education program could create more jobs. Could be both full and part-time. I haven't come up with a total for those. But if we get the influx of higher end residents we'd also need service people to support them."

Mark raised his hand. "I have another question."

The mayor laughed. "This is great. Look at us. Raising hands and asking questions just like at school. Go on, Mark. Ask your question."

"Are jobs the only measure of success? I mean, think about it. Redley's concerned with jobs. She says she's providing an economic use of the building. I'm wondering now," Mark paused, considering his words. He looked out the window.

"I hadn't thought about this before. That grant is supposed to have a community impact and you keep talking about an economic problem. Do we want to be considering something in addition to jobs in terms of solving our economic problem?"

Redley jumped in. "At first I was wondering if you were asking a real question or just challenging me. Now I see what you're wondering. Why haven't we talked about this sooner? What else economically do we need to be looking at?"

"Tax base," said the mayor.

"Wouldn't that be a function of property values?" asked Fletcher. "What about per capita income?"

They worked for a short time longer before the mayor stopped them. "Have to stop us for today. Our time's up. This was a good discussion but we've got a long ways to go." He turned to Julia. "Could you come back for our next meeting on Thursday?" He glanced back at the group. "Shall we have her at all our meetings?"

Fletcher jumped up impatiently and put on his coat. "I don't think so, Mayor. We wasted a lot of time with interruptions. Now I have another meeting to get to." He nodded to everyone, shoved his papers into his briefcase, and left.

Redley and Mark both urged the mayor to bring Julia back to their meetings, then said their good-byes.

Mayor White and Julia walked back to his office.

"Asking a question is such a little thing," said Cesar, slowing his steps as he thought. "When I called you I was hoping for more concrete help than that." He looked down at her.

"You'd be surprised, Mayor. I believe if the only thing I did was get people to ask more questions, all our interactions would improve."

"But…" He frowned but didn't finish the thought.

"Look," said Julia. "It was an important place to start for your team. If you had a team that always wandered off topic, I might have suggested they try a tightly scheduled agenda."

"I do feel kind of blind that I didn't notice they weren't asking any questions," said Cesar.

"It's part of that refocusing your lens I talked about before," said Julia. "It's a skill you can practice. You're so busy with content. The grant money. The mill building. The jobs. Even with all that, you noticed they were stating their opinions a lot, right?"

"Sure! It was driving me crazy. I just didn't know what to do about it."

"Now that you've started looking, you'll notice other things, too."

The mayor shrugged. "I don't know. They listened better today, but I've got a tight deadline. And I'm not going to fail!" He shook his head. "I'm going to need more help than that."

Pause and Reflect

Good leaders make sure to take time to pause and reflect, and schedule thinking time for themselves. The blank pages appearing irregularly throughout the book are your cue to pause and reflect. Take a moment to think about what you've been reading, what you've learned, and how it applies to you.

Chapter 4

Redley walked into her office slowly, hanging her down jacket on the antique horned coat rack in the corner, almost without seeing it even though it was her favorite yard sale find. She went to her window and watched the clouds fly across the grey sky in the wind.

"Boss Lady."

A voice interrupted her reverie. She turned. "Huh?"

Her assistant, Sam, was standing at her desk. "Boy, I could have driven a truck through here and you wouldn't have noticed. What's up? Bad meeting?"

She tilted her head and thought a minute. "No. No, it wasn't. It started out to be worse than usual with Fletcher taking charge. But then it went a lot better."

Sam rolled his eyes. "Mr. Suit and Tie? So what changed? Did he leave?"

Redley laughed and shook her head. "No, there was this consultant the mayor brought in. It was pretty interesting." She looked at Sam intently. "Do I ask questions?"

Sam shrugged. "I don't know. I haven't thought about it. I guess. You ask when things are going to be done. Why things are late. That sort of thing."

"That's not the questions I mean," said Redley. "In meetings. Do I ask everyone's opinions? Do I get curious?"

"What are you talking about?"

"Just answer me, Sam. I'm asking you a question. Do I ask questions in meetings? Do I encourage you all to ask questions?"

"Since these questions feel like an inquisition, I don't think I want you to ask questions," he answered, but she just stood looking at him. "No, I guess you don't ask a lot of questions. You're mostly throwing out ideas. The rest of us just try to keep up. That's what you do. You come up with ideas."

"Hmmmm," said Redley, and she turned back to the window.

Sam shrugged. "Marketing meeting in twenty minutes. Ask all the questions you want."

Redley quickly sat down at her desk and pulled up the email about the marketing meeting. Then she typed away, ending up with twelve questions she could ask. She printed out the agenda and her questions and ran off to the meeting, grabbing coffee on the way.

The conference room was on the old lighting balcony of the theater. It looked down over the production floor through a wide glass window that used to be the catwalk to access the beam where the spotlights had once hung. The table was made of a reclaimed section of bowling alley flooring. Everyone was sitting around it when she entered.

Redley sat down at the end of the table where the arrows that indicated the pin set up were inlaid, dark mahogany against the lighter heart pine narrow strips of the flooring.

"Before we get started, I would like your opinion. Do I ask a lot of questions?"

The marketing team looked around at each other and shrugged. The graphic artist spoke up.

"You don't ask questions. You're always giving your opinions. Real direct. No fooling around. You just say it like it is. We don't waste any time that way."

Redley was taken aback. "I don't ask what you think?"

He shook his head, his dreadlocks swinging. "Not really. I figure you assume we don't show you something unless we like it so you don't bother to ask."

Redley looked around the table. "Is that true for all of you?"

Everyone nodded their heads.

"Now, can we begin?" asked Stan, the marketing director.

Redley sighed. "Sure."

She made a point of totally keeping her opinions to herself. She took every chance she could to ask a question. The meeting seemed to go on forever. At the end she was as tight as a drum.

Stan asked if he could walk her back to her office. "What's up?" he asked. "You got a problem with the new marketing campaign?"

Redley slowed down and shook her head. "No, it's fine."

"Humph," said Stan. "I don't get what's going on. You don't seem yourself."

"That's a statement, Stan. Did you mean to ask a question?" asked Redley, obviously pleased with herself for prompting him to ask a question.

Stan sighed and frowned. "No. No, I guess I didn't." He stopped walking at her side, turning back toward his office. "If you're all set with the campaign, I've got lots to do."

Redley watched him walk away. "I've got to talk to Julia," she mumbled. "I'm clearly not getting this right."

Mark ran in through the back door of the clinic, hung up his coat and checked in with his nurse. He had four patients waiting. He sighed, washed his hands, and took up the first chart. It was an hour before he even had time for coffee.

"Hi Doc," said Melissa, his bookkeeper, when he walked back to the kitchen. She was making coffee. "Want some?" she asked, pointing to the pot.

"Definitely," he said. "This day is going to be a long one. I started out early over at the town hall and I'm already way behind."

"We're behind in another way, too. It's causing a problem. A big one."

"What now?" Mark asked.

"I just found out that because all the patient records aren't getting completed on time, the new software isn't sending the data to the billing company. Bills haven't gone out."

Mark's whole body went rigid. He bit at his lip until the words burst out of him. "What the hell?" he yelled. "Why didn't I know about this? Someone should have told me before this!" Melissa took a step back and opened her mouth then shut it. He stormed down the corridor and into his office, slamming the door hard enough that one of the Equal Employment Opportunity posters fell from the kitchen wall.

Minutes later, he was in front of Melissa's desk, running his hand over his chin in embarrassment. "Listen. I know this billing problem isn't your fault."

Melissa looked at him quietly for a long minute, then she nodded.

Someone tapped his shoulder. It was his nurse pointing down the hallway toward the examining rooms.

~~~~~~~~~~

Fletcher walked into his office. As soon as he had his coat off, Angie came to his door.

"Meeting any better today?" she asked

Fletcher shrugged. "That remains to be seen."

"Can I talk to you?"

"If it's not urgent, I need to return these calls." He pointed to the pile of messages on his desk.

"No, I guess. Not really urgent."

Fletcher nodded and picked up his phone, not even waiting for Angie to go back to her desk. He got involved in the calls and before he knew it, it was twelve thirty. Angie was gone to lunch.

She stopped into his office when she returned but he was on his way to a loan committee meeting.

"I can't talk now. Get me the Carson Chevrolet folder, will you Angie, while I print out Bob's notes."

She handed him the folder as he rushed by her desk. "Can we talk when you get back?"

He nodded, just pausing long enough to open the folder and check that it was complete. When he came back his three o'clock appointment with the private banking client was waiting in the lobby. Angie ushered the elderly man in a dated three-piece suit into Fletcher's office and offered coffee. When she brought it back they were deep in conversation.

After the gentleman left, Fletcher opened his computer to check emails. Angie knocked at his door frame.

"I've got to leave early to pick up my daughter," she said. "Do you have time for just one quick question?"

"Of course," said Fletcher, as he finished typing the sentence. "Just let me finish this email."

She stood waiting two more minutes until he finally looked up. She took a deep breath before she spoke and her words came out rapidly. "Mr. Harrington, do you think I do a good job for you? I mean." She flushed. "I'm not fishing for compliments. I just need to know."

"If you weren't doing a good job, you'd know it. You don't need me to tell you that."

He glanced back down at his computer screen.

"Right," she said. She started buttoning her coat as she nodded and turned. "Right."

Fletcher shook his head. "What do people want these days," he said to himself. He went back to his email.

She came back in with her purse slung over her shoulder and her gloves on. She handed him an envelope.

"Here," she said. "This is for you."

"What is it?" he asked, turning the plain envelope over. It was sealed. "Where did this come from?"

"It's from me. It's my letter of resignation."

Fletcher looked up quickly, pushed his chair away from the desk and stood. "What do you mean? Angie? What's this about?"

"I need to go. My daughter's waiting outside the school and it's cold. This is what I wanted to talk to you about earlier today. And the other day, too. But you didn't have time."

"But why? Angie, I need you. You're the best assistant I ever had."

"You never told me that. Never."

"I didn't need to. It was obvious." Fletcher leaned down to pull a folder out of the file drawer of his desk. "Your raise was above the percent for anyone else who's had this role."

"Look, I have to go. It's not about the money, anyway."

"Wait. What do you mean it isn't about money? We're a bank. We're all about money. Do you hate the job?"

"No! Mr. Harrington, I've worked for you for over a year. Do you know in all that time you've never asked me anything about myself or my life?"

"That's your personal business. I'd be intruding."

"Well, you never even asked me if I liked the job. That's not intruding."

"That's true," he agreed. "But it can't just be that. If it's not the pay, it's the hours. You have another job, right?"

"No! It's not the pay, or the hours. Or the work. It's that I've never gotten to, you know, to feel like a person. Feel appreciated."

"Of course I appreciate you!" he said with frustration. "It's obvious."

"That's what I mean. You assume I know these things. How would I know? You say hello in the morning. Goodbye in the evening. Other than that we never have a conversation about anything except the work you need from me."

"I don't…" He stumbled into an awkward silence.

"If we worked in different departments that would be fine. But I sit outside your office." Angie waved toward her desk. "Right out there. It just feels strange to me. I've had enough."

"It feels strange to you," he repeated. He ran his fingers through his thin gray hair. "I'm not good at this. I don't get what you want."

"Take time to read my letter. I'm not leaving you high and dry. I'm giving you plenty of notice." Angie was backing away, obviously anxious to leave.

"No, no." Fletcher jumped up and strode across the room, pushing the letter into her hand. "You keep the letter. We'll talk more tomorrow. Don't do anything rash."

She looked at the envelope he had pushed into her hand, took it, and tossed it on her desk as she walked out.

Chapter 5

On Thursday, when Fletcher arrived at the conference room, Redley and Mark were already seated at the table.

"Aren't we all the early birds?" he said as he hung up his raincoat.

"I came early to try to talk with the consultant about that question thing she mentioned Tuesday. I tried it at a meeting and maybe caused myself some people problems," admitted Redley.

Fletcher sat down with a scowl on his face and clicked open his briefcase. He took out a file and set the briefcase on the floor heavily. "People problems. Yeah!"

"What's your issue, Fletch?" asked Redley, curiously.

"I don't have an issue," he answered. "Everything at my bank is fine. Just fine."

Redley shrugged and turned back to Mark.

"I just don't get what people want these days," Fletcher burst out. "Can't business just be business?"

Redley and Mark looked at each other in surprise.

"I work with my assistant every day. I give her a great raise. She's still unhappy because... because... I don't even know why. I asked her again this morning. She says I don't know anything about her. If she wants me to know something, why doesn't she tell me?"

Mark shook his head. "I think I have the opposite problem. I get so interested in people I'm always running late."

"See. That's why business should be about business," said Fletcher.

"Good morning," said Julia as she came in. She took off her coat, shaking the water off it and draping it over the back of a chair. She sat down and slowly scanned the frowning faces around the table. No one responded. She smoothed the skirt of her suit.

"Great red scarf," commented Redley.

Julia thanked her.

They all sat in silence.

"It seems I interrupted you," said Julia, starting to get up. "I can wait in the hall if you prefer."

"Fletcher was just complaining about his assistant quitting," said Redley, before she was stared down by Fletcher.

"I didn't say she quit," said Fletcher.

"Oh dear," said Julia. "Sounds like a problem."

"Of course it is! I need her. I want her to stay working with me." Fletcher drummed his fingers on the file in front of him. "I thought everything was fine," he muttered, more to himself than to the group. "You tell me," he said finally, turning to Julia, "since you claim to know so much about people's behavior. What on earth does she want?"

"I don't know," said Julia. "Have you asked her?"

"She just says I don't appreciate her. I gave her a big raise. I don't get it."

"For some people," said Julia, "it's not about the…"

"Don't tell me it's not about money," interrupted Fletcher. "That's what she said. It's always about the money, even for Redley and Mark, here, if they'd admit it. You only pay more when you value something. I give her a good raise. Ipso facto, I value her. She should know that." He nodded his head.

Redley just raised her eyebrows.

"What?" asked Fletcher.

"Clearly, she doesn't," said Mark, squinting slightly into the distance. "You know, Fletcher," he said, "I tell my patients all the time. Work, family, either way. Relationships take some effort."

"I don't want to treat her like family. I have a family," complained Fletcher. "Even Julia can't tell me I should treat her like family."

"That's not what it means," said Redley. "But you do have to start becoming aware of what she wants."

"I can't go around being aware all the time. I have things to do. Work to get done," argued Fletcher.

"Think about your customers," Julia suggested quietly. "Doing work when it involves other people requires awareness, doesn't it?"

Redley nodded. She reminded Fletcher that the bank's advertising was all about building relationships and knowing the customer.

"Of course," said Fletcher. "Of course we know our customers."

"So does that change how you work with them?" asked Julia.

"Look, let's forget this. Where's the mayor?" asked Fletcher.

"He'll be here," said Redley. "Go on, Julia. I want to hear this myself."

"Okay, let's go back to the customer. Do you behave differently with each of them, depending on what you know about them? Fletcher, I'll bet you wear a suit jacket with some customers and not always with others."

"He never puts his jacket on when I come in," laughed Redley.

"He puts it on for me," said Mark, thoughtfully.

"Okay. So why do you do that, Fletcher?" asked Julia.

"Redley's informal," said Fletcher quickly. "Mark is a bit older. He's a doctor. It just feels appropriate to put my jacket on."

Julia smiled and nodded. "That's one way of noticing how each customer is different."

"Of course they're different," said Fletcher impatiently. "I tell all our employees to pay attention to how they're different, to get to know their customers, know about their families, their businesses. That's part of our orientation training."

"Right," Julia said. "That's what builds the basis to work together. That builds the relationship."

"With some more than others." Fletcher grimaced. "These days you can know everything about them and have the best relationship in the world and they still run to another bank for a quarter percent interest."

"Okay, but others don't leave," objected Redley. "Look at me. At this point, I could go elsewhere for that quarter percent. But I stay for two reasons. Because you took a chance when I was small and because you offer what I need. You know what I need and you get it done. Right?"

Fletcher nodded. "Glad you think so," he said, almost smiling. He turned back to Julia. "Maybe I get Redley because she's a business person. But my assistant...."

"It does get harder to figure out," said Julia, "when we value different things. Like you and your assistant."

Fletcher sighed.

"You care more about getting things done," said Julia. "That's valuing the strategic piece."

Fletcher nodded emphatically, as did Redley.

"I'm guessing that your assistant cares about the relationships."

Mark nodded.

"I call that the relational work. Some people call it the intimate piece," said Julia with a grin. "People always remember that."

Fletcher grimaced. "What?"

Julia laughed. "Not that kind of intimate. It's the sense of the human in you seeing the human in her and visa versa. You know. Like the way your staff gets to know something about your customers' families. Or their hobbies. Not just because you have to but because you're interested. It builds trust. You can't get much done as a leader without trust."

"That's what I do with my patients," said Mark. "Sometimes I get asked why I still take people's blood pressure when I have a nurse do it first. I know it's old school but it's a way for me to initiate touch. To step closer to them. I think it helps them trust me."

Redley looked at him curiously. "I always wondered about that," she said.

"Still and all," commented Fletcher. "In my business, things have to get done."

Julia nodded. "Absolutely. You can't only have the relational connection between people; you need the strategic as well. That's true everywhere. Mark can't only empathize with his patients, he has to treat them."

"In fact," added Mark, "getting to know them helps me treat them. Sometimes it's a diagnostic clue. I found out about a case of domestic abuse last week because of the conversation we were having about their dog. I had no idea. I just like dogs."

Julia pursed her lips and nodded. "It's even true in families. You have to get things done there, too. Deciding where to go on vacation. Budgeting. Getting your kids to do their homework. All kinds of strategic things."

"I don't have much luck on the homework front so let's stick with business," said Fletcher, looking at his watch. "Speaking of which, what's keeping the mayor? It's not like him to be late."

"I'll text him," said Redley, continuing to speak as her fingers flew across her phone. "It's like you always say about customers, Fletcher. People do business with people they know."

"So are you telling me I should treat her like a customer?" asked Fletcher. "Is that the bottom line?"

"Probably would be the best thing that happened to her," said Redley, looking up. "Your bank is known for customer service. What if you thought of her that way?"

"You should have just said that to begin with," said Fletcher.

The door opened suddenly, and the mayor rushed in. "Let's get to work," he barked.

"Can you give us a few more minutes, Chief?" asked Redley. "We're almost done here. Mark and I had a few more questions for Julia."

"Done? How can you be done? I haven't even called us to order." The mayor frowned and threw his papers on the table.

"Hey, don't get your panties in a wad, Chief," responded Redley. "This wasn't meeting stuff. Fletcher was just asking Julia for some help with a personal problem."

"Just see here. I never asked for help," said Fletcher. "And it was business, not personal."

Redley grinned and linked two fingers together, holding them out to Fletcher.

"Mayor," said Mark. "Since we don't have a lot of time together, maybe Julia could work with all of us individually, as well as work with the committee."

"What the hell's going on here? Last week you didn't want any help." Cesar dragged the chair from the table so roughly it fell to the floor. "Damn it!"

"We're learning something," said Redley, after he'd picked up the chair and settled himself. "I want to learn more. In fact, we need to learn more for this whole grant to come through."

"I don't have this in my budget," the mayor snapped. "In fact, you know I barely have Julia's fee in my budget. Now we're wasting time and money."

"I'll chip in," said Redley, abruptly.

"I will, too," said Mark.

"No!" The mayor slammed his hand on the table.

"Whoa," said Redley. "What's the problem, Chief?"

"I had a reporter sniffing around my office just this morning. Asked pointed questions about how long we're taking. I know this guy, just looking for dirt. The last thing I need is for him to start writing about me hiring consultants for everyone in town. This guy's trouble!"

Chapter 6

The room was silent until finally Julia filled the void.

"So does that frame the agenda for this meeting, Mayor?" she asked.

"I was here late last night with contract negotiations. Then that damn reporter this morning. I guess we keep on hashing things out," he answered. "We just need to get to a decision."

"I agree," said Fletcher. "You know, if we make the decision for the cultural center today, we could start having plans drawn and work on the narrative for the grant, and then..."

"But..." interrupted Redley. "We could do the same if we decided on a business incubator."

"Mayor, I wonder if you'd allow me to interrupt for a minute," said Julia.

"Yes, right. Someone ask a question," Cesar said, frowning.

"Well, yes, that's right and I'm glad you brought it up," said Julia, "but actually I was going to mention something else first. You see, good meetings have a natural cycle."

Julia got up and walked quickly to the flip chart and drew a wave form diagram. "To keep it simple today, think of it as a beginning, middle, and a good ending. The focus is fuzzy at first as everyone arrives from whatever else they were doing and shifts gears to the topic of the meeting."

She turned and tapped the beginning of the wave form. Fletcher rolled his eyes. Julia continued on. "Here, at the beginning, the leader encourages the team to connect with each other and frames up the issues to deal with."

"You wanted questions? Here's a question," said Fletcher. "Why should we spend time on connecting when we all know each other?"

Redley laughed. "You of all people shouldn't be asking that. Didn't you learn anything from Angie?"

"I'm in Fletcher's camp," said the mayor. "We don't need that. We all know each other. We just need to get things done."

"Look at it this way," said Julia, still standing at the flip chart. "You'll find the work goes better if you take a few minutes to… to sort of get into sync. Like musicians arriving at a concert and starting to tune up. When you all come into the meeting room you're coming from different places, different agendas, with different thoughts on your mind."

Mark nodded. "Like the mayor here coming in when we were in the midst of a different conversation."

Julia nodded. "Right. Mayor, you came in with a lot on your mind. You're in a very different place than the rest of your team. So for just a few minutes you could have everyone check in, how they're doing, what's on their mind, anything the group needs to know."

"Actually," said Mark, "I may be getting an emergency call which I'll have to take, so my phone here is on vibrate."

"A patient?" Redley asked.

Mark shook his head a bit sheepishly. "No, my dog."

"Oh, Mark, I'm sorry," said Redley. "That big old teddy bear?"

"Ate a chicken bone. They tend to splinter. May need surgery to remove it or it may pass through. That's what I'm waiting to hear."

Redley patted Mark's arm. "I know he's part of your family."

Julia nodded. "That's what I mean. Checking in, connecting, taking care of any personal business. Think of those musicians tuning up together. Preparing themselves individually and as a group. Then, the leader reviews the meeting agenda."

"Too much time, Ms. Breuer," said the mayor, sounding more and more impatient. "We may not have an agenda today, but we do have a lot to cover."

"Still, you'll find the work goes better if you take a few minutes to frame up clear expectations for your team, connect the dots from the last meeting, frame up the purpose of this meeting—is it information sharing, exploring and brainstorming for new ideas, challenging an assumption, reaching consensus." She quickly wrote each item within the box on the flip chart as she went along. "That allows each individual to join in your goal. Provides clarity," finished Julia. "You need to establish clarity..."

"Enough!" Cesar slammed his hand on the table and everyone jumped.

Nancy Hardaway

Pause and Reflect

Chapter 7

"I don't need or want a lecture, Ms. Breuer!" The mayor stood up, his black mustache covering his tight lips. "I've been a very successful leader for a long time. I don't need you to take over today."

"You're right," said Julia, carefully setting down the marker and returning to her seat.

"This is my committee," said the mayor.

"Absolutely."

"We have work to do. This isn't your classroom. I have a meeting to run here."

"Yes, of course you do. I'm sorry it felt that way."

An awkward silence filled the room.

"Come on, Mayor," said Mark. "You hired Julia to give us help. She's giving us help. Isn't that okay? I don't think she was ever trying to run the meeting."

The mayor just glared at Mark.

"No, Mark," said Julia softly. "The mayor is right. I started to lecture. I understand why I did but that's not important."

"But why…" started Redley.

Julia touched her hand to stop her and turned to the mayor. "Thank you for telling me." She put her hands in her lap and sat quietly. When the mayor didn't say anything or even make eye contact she leaned toward him. "I wonder, is there something else?"

Mark's phone suddenly lit up and started vibrating. They all turned to look at the table where it sat. He picked it up, looked at the number and turned to the mayor questioningly.

"Take it, Mark," said the mayor. "We'll adjourn for a few minutes. Julia, I'll speak to you in private."

Julia nodded. "Absolutely."

She stood and followed him out of the room and down the hall. He stopped in an alcove away from any doors.

"That's my team in there, not yours," said the mayor, jabbing his finger past her toward the room. "Don't you ever treat me like I don't know anything in front of them."

"Yes, I can see how upset you are and I am very sorry for that, Mayor White." He was standing so close and she was so much smaller that she had to bend her head way back to see him.

"I don't like being humiliated," muttered the mayor.

"Is that what it felt like for you? That was certainly not my intent and I apologize. I got carried away trying to help. Clearly it was terribly clumsy of me."

"I didn't like it," said Cesar.

"Yes, I understand," agreed Julia.

"I'm not sure I feel comfortable working with you anymore."

"Oh dear," said Julia. "I can see you might feel that way. I appreciate your honesty. Did you feel that way last meeting, too?"

Cesar shifted his weight from one foot to the other, his hand rattling the change in his pocket. "No," he admitted. "That was fine. But today was unacceptable."

"Yes, I see that. I wonder, is there anything I can do now to make things better between us?" Julia asked softly.

"I don't know." Cesar looked away from Julia and down the hall where Mark was finishing his cell phone call and returning to the conference room. Julia waited. "I don't know," he repeated.

"Mayor, it is my goal as well as my role to support you in any way I can. I thought that was what I was doing, but I was too heavy-handed. I made a mistake. It was unintentional, but I imagine that doesn't change the way it felt to you?"

The mayor just shook his head.

"So what should we do now? Would you like me to leave?" asked Julia, finally. "I can recommend a replacement. Or I'm sure your mother-in-law can find you someone else."

Cesar looked down at Julia, then away. They stood without speaking, the jingling change in his pocket the only noise.

Finally he spoke. "You're reminding me of something my mother-in-law said about you. She said 'Cesar, this woman is direct, and intent on helping her clients. Knowing you, at times you may not like her. Just remember she does amazing things with teams and leaders.'"

He looked down at her, still frowning. "I don't want to waste any more of the group's time. Let's go back in."

"I understand there's more here. Can you talk further after the meeting?" she asked.

He shook his head. "Back to back meetings. Look, let it go. We'll move on."

He turned and walked back to the meeting room and opened the door, holding it while she walked in and took her seat. Redley, Mark, and Fletcher all watched in awkward silence.

"Mark, how's the dog?" asked the mayor.

"All set. Sorry to have interrupted."

The mayor nodded and took a deep breath. "Okay, let's get back to work. Let's sum up where we were when we ended last time. Then we'll decide together where we go from there."

They talked about the shift in the last meeting from talking about the building and its qualities to the larger problems in town.

"Look," said the mayor. "I have an idea. Let's do things a little different today. We can see if we could finish up that discussion by coming to a shared vision of what we want for the town."

Redley looked interested. "So we create a picture of what we want this town to look like and feel like in the future. You know, when this project, whatever it is, is a success. What the benefits will be?"

Mark was quick to endorse the idea.

Fletcher took off his glasses and nodded. "It's worth a shot." He clicked the ends of his glasses together. "With new bank products we look at features and benefits. That's what you're talking about."

"Good," said the mayor. "How about you start, Mark."

"Sure. For me, the town would look like it used to look. With an active, healthy, community spirit. Kids playing at the park on the village green. People walking down the sidewalk on Main Street. All the stores full. An active community."

"What else does an active community look like?" the mayor asked. Julia nodded.

"That families are here. They'll connect with each other and bring their friends from elsewhere because they'll have a good quality of life."

"I've got a question. What does that mean, Mark?" asked Redley. "What do you think of as a good quality of life?"

"Safety. Support from one another. Shared values. They'll have kids here. That they stay here instead of leaving. That they grow and prosper. They're going to say things like, 'I'm going to open a restaurant in that empty storefront where there was a diner before.' They're going to step forward and do that sort of thing. Take initiative to build this town back up."

"That's great, Mark. So what about you, Redley?" asked the mayor.

"Let's see." She closed her eyes for a minute then pushed her sleeves up and sat forward in her chair. "New businesses opening up. Start ups that grow successful here. Job postings. People moving in. Perhaps some new business programs at the college."

"What about the feel of the town?" asked Mark.

"Hmmm. Good question," said Redley, then she started ticking ideas off on her fingers. "Coffee shops where people go and have meetings and work at their computers and run into each other and spark more new ideas and collaborations. New trendy restaurants serving local food. Our great seafood, and the organic farm produce that now gets shipped out because there's not enough demand and people here can't afford it anyway. Young professionals playing Ultimate Frisbee in leagues and bringing their friends for the quality of life and staying to settle and have families here. Kayaks on the river. Vibrant. Fun. Alive." She was grinning with excitement.

"I like that picture. You've added some color and details to what I said," observed Mark, smiling. "We're not seeing it much differently, are we?"

Redley nodded. "You're right. Not really. Wouldn't it be awesome?"

"What about you, Fletcher?" asked Mark. "What's your picture of our future?"

"Interesting question. Desirability, I guess," said Fletcher.

"Can you be more specific about what you're seeing?" asked Mark.

"Sure. Let's see. A viable cultural life for all of us. Older professionals wanting to move out of the big metropolitan areas. Then new, small professional firms like trust and estate firms and insurance companies opening to support them. Investment firms, maybe. Followed by restaurants and specialty boutiques that would serve the older professionals and be opened by younger entrepreneurs. Main Street windows full. Lots of new jobs for young people who'd want to settle here permanently and raise families, because of the quality of our schools." He looked around.

They continued to talk and question each other about details with great animation, until finally the mayor stood up.

"Let's stay with the big picture." He made a list on the flip chart, stating them out loud as he wrote. "Restaurants. Community. Sports. New jobs. Young entrepreneurs. Older professionals. Vibrant Main Street. Do I have that right?" He finished the list then turned around then tapped his marker on the flip chart. They all nodded. "You've drawn the picture I've had for this town since I took office. Why I wanted to be mayor. For the first time we have agreement. It's about time!"

He sat back down and looked at his watch. "I wonder if this isn't the place to finish for today." He deliberately turned to Julia. "I believe you said something about good endings?"

Pause and Reflect

Chapter 8

J ulia responded quickly, though she showed a hint of surprise. "I did. Good meetings leave time for good endings."

"What is it you want us to do?" asked Fletcher, with an awkward smile. "Not hold hands and sing?"

Julia raised one eyebrow. "It wouldn't be my choice."

"Nor mine!" said Cesar. "You don't want to hear me sing. So what now, Julia?"

"I was referring," said Julia, "to taking a few minutes to sum up and evaluate what you've done together, make sure you agree on any decisions, talk about next steps."

Redley looked thoughtful. "Like that list up there the Chief just made for us?"

"Yes," agreed Julia. "He's already begun the process."

"You know," Redley said, turning to Fletcher, "you keep putting down everything Julia says. What about that orchestra example she gave us earlier about the importance of good beginnings? Did that mean anything to you?"

"Actually, yes," said Fletcher, as if he couldn't bear admitting it.

"Why?" asked Redley.

He shrugged. "I like listening to that process of tuning up. In fact, I'm always in my seat early because I find it so compelling."

Redley looked at Fletcher in surprise. "You do? What do you find compelling about it?"

Fletcher sighed reluctantly. "Seeing and hearing their preparation allows me to prepare myself. They chat with each other. Then they start tuning. As I watch and listen, it helps me to be ready to hear the music when the lights dim."

"Wow," said Redley. "That's cool. I never thought about it. I'll pay more attention next time I go to the symphony."

"You? You go to the symphony?" asked Fletcher. "Ha!"

"Look, don't treat me like a cultural infidel. I like all kinds of music. I go to the symphony. I had season tickets one year when I lived in Boston."

Fletcher looked as if he were seeing her for the first time. The mayor glanced from one to the other with equal surprise.

"So think about endings the same way," said Julia. "What would it be like if at the end of the symphony, before the last note was even silent, the curtain came down and immediately the lights came up and we just rushed out? No poignant silence after the last crescendo, no bows. No applause. No conversation with friends."

"It would be really weird. Unfinished," said Redley. "But I have to admit that's often how my meetings end."

Fletcher nodded slowly. "I've always got a long agenda. There's just too much to do. Then I usually have another meeting to rush off to."

"Okay, so we agree it's important, so let's try to finish quickly, but finish well," said Cesar. "I'll sum up by saying I'm glad and relieved that we finally reached agreement on something."

"Ditto," said Redley. "I'm actually excited about what could happen here. I mean, it's really pretty cool if we could pull all this off."

"It certainly would be a highly successful return on investment for the town," said Fletcher. "And the bank," he added.

"I don't know all of what it will take," said Mark, "but it's invigorating to talk about what this town could be. It gives me a sense of possibility. Makes me want to come back for our next meeting, rather than dreading it." He shrugged. "Sorry about that, Mayor, but you know. This is a shift for me."

Cesar grinned. "Julia, anything to add?" he asked her, expansively.

"Just something to be aware of," she said. "All four of you spoke about your vision of the future, and at the same time stayed curious about one another's ideas. Your questions helped you see you have a common vision to act on." She nodded. "Good meeting, Mayor."

"We do, and we will," Cesar said as he stood. "But I usually think of this as a committee of three. Their committee."

"You have a vote, don't you?" asked Redley. "We need a unanimous vote of the four of us. You could veto whatever we come up with, even if we all agreed, right?"

Pause and Reflect

Chapter 9

Cesar walked into his house through the back door to the kitchen. "Something smells good, Kelly," he said, leaning over and kissing his wife as she worked at the desk tucked into a windowed alcove. "What'd you make?"

"I'm just reheating the beef lentil soup you made last weekend that we froze."

He laughed. "I guess I like the taste of my own cooking. Can I get you anything?"

She patted his ample belly. "Of course you like your own cooking. You always have. And sure. I'll have a very light Old-Fashioned."

"Putting me to work, tonight, huh?" he asked as he opened the liquor cabinet over the microwave.

He hummed a bit off key as he sliced oranges, spooned out cherries, and shook bitters onto two sugar cubes he had placed in each glass. After adding the bourbon, he filled both glasses with ice. By the time he put away the fixings, she had turned off her computer.

"So, how was the Blue Ribbon Committee? You sound like you're in a good mood. Is Julia helping?" she asked as she took the glass he handed her.

He leaned against her desk and considered. "I'm not sure. I had to put her in her place today."

"You what?" Kelly started up from her chair.

"She was starting to take over!"

"What do you mean, take over? That can't be right."

"She was taking over my meeting," said Cesar, annoyance clear in his voice. "That's not her role. And what do you mean that can't be right?"

"What do you mean taking over?" Kelly asked again.

"Look, even she agreed."

"Agreed to what? You're not... Did she take over your agenda?"

"No, but the group was all talking to her rather than me. Then it was like we couldn't take a step without her. She was talking too much. Getting in the way. So I took her to task."

"Isn't she supposed to give advice? How does she do that without talking?"

"She lectured me! All right?" His dark bushy eyebrows met over his eyes.

"You are so sensitive," muttered Kelly.

"What d'you mean, sensitive?"

She shrugged. "You hate feedback."

"Why are you attacking me?"

She laughed and took a sip of her drink. "I'm not going to fight you about it. Isn't there a Shakespeare quote. 'He who protests too much,' right?"

"Yeah, so what does that mean? You're supposed to be on my side, remember?"

"Of course I'm on your side," Kelly said, reaching out to take his hand.

"So fine. I hate feedback. You don't like feedback, either."

"Depends. I listen when people tell me something that teaches me something."

Cesar pulled his hand away. "She was scolding me. Not teaching me. I didn't want to hear that. Not in front of the others. Plus, she's supposed to help the whole team, not just me."

"Ahhh. So it's about your ego." Her warm smile softened the words.

Cesar looked down at this half empty glass, swirling the drink around and reaching in with his fingers for an ice cube. "Let's get back to Julia."

"Fine. You said you put her in her place? Did she get angry? Poor woman with you and your temper coming down on her. Look, sit down. The soup can wait. Tell me what happened. What will my mother say when she hears?"

"No. I'm hungry. Let's eat now. And this isn't about your mother. Don't drag her into this. Besides, I'm not the only

one in this house with a temper. Seems to me last week Miss
Irish Lassy tore the refrigerator repairman apart."

Kelly laughed ruefully, and raised her drink to him. "Too
true."

"Plus, Julia Breuer may be tiny, but you don't have to feel
sorry for her. She's no push-over. She's tough. And wily."
Cesar laughed and took a big sip of what was left of his drink.
"I have to hand it to her. Now let's eat."

When they were sitting over dinner, the mayor told his wife
the story more slowly. "She basically described a good meeting
structure. What a good beginning of a meeting would look
like. The meeting had already begun. I felt scolded…"

He reached out for more soup and re-filled his bowl. "What
the hell. She was probably right. It's just my back's against a
wall with this deadline." He sighed.

"What did she say? Did she defend herself?"

"No. Didn't defend herself. Not at all, come to think of it.
No, she just sat there. In fact, she actually leaned in toward
me and asked if I had anything else I wanted to say to her.
That impressed me. I expected her to argue back at me."

Kelly watched her husband. She could see him replaying
the interchange in his mind.

Cesar took a piece of bread and slathered it with butter. "I
probably would have blown my top if she'd tried to argue.
Instead, she asked me questions like she really wanted to
know where I stood. I guess that kept me from going off in
a tirade."

"Interesting. Should I try that?" Kelly asked, a playful smile
on her face.

Cesar tilted his head and grinned. "You probably should,
my dear. On second thought, you do it anyway. You, of all
people, are familiar with my tirades, sorry to say. I'm just
lucky you rarely take them seriously."

She laughed as she got up and kissed him on the cheek
before picking up his empty dishes. "I knew you had your
father's temper when I married you. I fell for your hot Latin
looks and your hot blooded passion for life."

"And I fell for your white Irish skin and your adorable freckles and your damn smart mouth." He grabbed her around the waist and took the dishes out of her hand, demonstrating just how passionate he was. When he released her, she grinned.

They took the dishes to the kitchen. A little while later they sat down at the table with milk and cookies.

"So, really, Cesar. Is Julia doing anything for you? For the team? I mean, you know you don't have to have her keep coming if she isn't. Mother won't be offended."

He dunked his cookie in the glass of milk. "I can't run this town to please your mother," he said, his words garbled as he chewed. "I think something might be helping. I'm not sure yet."

"Like how?" asked Kelly, dunking her own cookie in her milk.

"We were all pretty discouraged."

"I know you were."

"The other three were worse. You know I'm optimistic. Plus it's my job. They're volunteers."

"So are they still discouraged?" asked Kelly.

"No. That's it. I don't think so. Not as much, anyway. Julia pointed out that we aren't a total mess as a team. Gotten us to see ourselves a little differently."

"Like what?" Kelly got up and put more cookies on their plates.

"That we're all passionate about the town. I knew that, obviously, but somehow having it said aloud made it more important. That it's a skill to be able to all be strong at stating our opinions. We weren't paying attention to it. Took it for granted, I guess."

"Makes sense."

"So she's encouraging us to ask questions."

"Ask questions?"

Cesar described the idea of adding in the opposite of what they were doing. "You're good at asking questions. Probably what makes you such a good fund raiser. You're really curious about what's important to people. Rather than jam a cause down people's throats, you just noodle around long enough in their heads to see if there's a match."

"Geez. That makes it sound pretty sneaky," she said, wrinkling her nose. "Like subliminal advertising. I don't get in their heads. I do get interested, though."

"That's what I mean. We were getting into the gimmick of the question, but it's more about getting interested. For the first time today, I think they really got interested in what each other had to say, and started to discover how to work together."

"So if things are better, what did she do that you're complaining about?" asked Kelly.

Cesar explained Julia's comments about how it's important for good meetings to create connection between the people and clarity about the agenda at the beginning, then summarize at the end to review decisions and next steps. As he finished he started to laugh.

"It makes sense now that I repeat it. I couldn't listen at the time. I was just too irritated." He shook his head, still chuckling. "You know, by the end, she actually got them to say they were excited."

"That's progress."

"Still, we need a decision," Cesar said. "And fast. That reporter was sniffing around my office again talking to staff. You know the one. From my campaign?"

"Uh-oh," said Kelly, frowning.

"Uh-oh is right."

"He's back? Where's he working this time? I liked it when he was off the radar. Didn't he make enough trouble during your campaign?"

"He says he's got a new online column. I guess I should check it out."

"What's he want?" asked Kelly, her voice tinged dark by anger and concern.

"I'm not sure. That's what worries me. I think he's still trying to be the big investigative reporter. Why would anyone hire him? He doesn't care about facts as long as his story is sensational."

Pause and Reflect

Chapter 10

Two days later, the mayor was sitting at his desk checking his email before the team meeting when he heard a soft knock. It was Julia Breuer. She stood at the door and they chatted for a moment about the weather.

"I'm here early to check-in with you," she said. "I want to apologize again for upsetting you at our last meeting. I was into my teaching and not sensitive to you."

"Well...." said the mayor. "It was awkward," he admitted.

She nodded.

"Look," said Cesar, "I recognize that I asked for your help and then when you gave it, I rejected it."

"Entirely your prerogative. I've said for a long time that help isn't help unless it's helpful."

The mayor looked at her for a minute. "I think that makes sense in a cryptic sort of way. Can you say more?"

"Sure. I've always been in the business of helping people, one way or another. Obviously, I like to help. Sometimes, I get carried away. The only one that can judge whether my actions are helpful is the other person. Not me. In our case, you're the only one who really knows whether or not I'm helpful. I need to be more aware of that. Which I wasn't being."

"Hmmmm," said Cesar. He sat quietly for a moment, then reached over and held up the photo of his daughter. "You're reminding me. She used to say, 'DAD! You're not being helpful!'" He laughed out loud at the memory. "You know how many times I heard that?"

Julia's laughter joined his as she reached for the picture. "Absolutely. I still have to stop myself with my own children. They tell me to stop being a coach. It's just tough, right? Because the ones we care about most are the ones we most want to help."

Cesar nodded and they sat in companionable silence for a moment.

Julia handed him back the photo and pointed to the other picture on his desk. "Is that your son?" she asked.

The mayor picked up the framed photo taken of a big yellow raft navigating down a white water river. The two faces in the front of the raft were grinning from under their helmets. "That was taken two years ago. He gave that trip to me for my fiftieth birthday."

"Where does he live?" asked Julia. "Nearby?"

"No, unfortunately. This town has no opportunities for someone like him. He's an environmental scientist. He works on Cape Cod at the Woods Hole Oceanographic Institute."

"You must be proud."

"I am. You mentioned children?" asked Cesar.

"Both grown. My daughter directs a research department and writes on health care policy for the federal government. Lives on a farm with her family outside of Washington, D.C. My son's a physicist. He has a lab in San Diego. Also a huge studio there where he does metal sculpture."

"You must be proud," he said. He tilted his head and pressed his fingers together thoughtfully. "You came here on purpose, didn't you?"

She smiled. "Yes, of course. I couldn't leave things the way they were. We needed to clear the air, so to speak. Reconnect."

"Good." The mayor looked at her, then came around the desk and sat in the guest chair opposite her. "I'm sorry I was a bully the other day. I do need help," he said simply. "You said a good leader frames up the goal for the meeting but I don't know what to do next. Where the hell should we go? I should know, but I don't. I'm not used to not knowing."

"It's hard to get perspective when you're in the trenches, Mayor. That's why you call in help."

"Please, call me Cesar."

She nodded. "Cesar, remember what I said about paying attention to patterns?" He nodded but looked confused. "Do you like to dance?" she asked.

Chapter 11

"I don't dance like the young kids do," said Cesar. "My wife and I sometimes ballroom dance, but what does that have to do with anything?"

"Remember those rules I mentioned? It's the one about seeing from different perspectives. Stick with me for a minute. When you and your wife are on the dance floor, what do you notice?"

"Her face, her hair. The feel of her in my arms. Sometimes the steps if we're doing a dance we don't do often."

"Exactly. That's seeing close-up. Now imagine if the two of you left the room and went upstairs to a place you could look down on the dance floor. What might you see?"

"Let's see. The whole room. She might look at what all the other women were wearing. Colors? Who's a good dancer and who's bad?"

"Great. What else?" prompted Julia.

"Hmmmm. How many were on the dance floor, how many sitting it out. Where they are on the floor. Are they all bunched up at the back, maybe, if the band is playing too loud or are they spread out pretty evenly?"

She nodded. "Exactly. With the wide angle lens, you can see the patterns. Not just the details of you and the people right next to you, but the bigger patterns."

Cesar nodded quickly. "I get it. I'm on the dance floor with this damn committee. Looking through the close up lens. All I see is the decision looming and this team not getting anywhere. So what can I do to refocus?"

Pause and Reflect

Chapter 12

"Shifting your focus takes practice, and it takes intentional awareness, Cesar, and giving yourself some thinking time," said Julia. "Sometimes, just asking yourself how you might shift your focus can help you. What if you imagine yourself shifting to wide angle with your team? What do you see?"

"I've got the flip chart from last time," he said, pointing to his desk. He looked at it and then out the window as he thought. "Mostly before, we've been talking about the building itself and what we can do with it." He glanced back at the flip chart. "This last meeting we shifted. We spent all our time talking about our ideal vision for this town."

Julia nodded, and leaned forward a bit in her chair.

"So," Cesar went on, "we were looking at the future of the building and then the future of the town. Right?"

"Good observation. That's definitely a pattern."

"Okay, so what if we did the opposite? We could talk about the past, although I can't see that that makes any sense." Cesar shook his head. "Plus Redley wasn't even here." He drummed his fingers on the desk, rattling the flip chart. "We could talk about the present. But we all know it. We live here. We see it every day."

She nodded. "Of course you do. I wonder, though. Have you all talked about it together? As a committee? Talked about the impact on you and your families? Talked in detail together like you talked about your future vision?"

Cesar leaned on the edge of the desk and propped his chin on his hand, frowning. Finally he shook his head. "You know, you're right. We haven't talked about it in a serious way. Sure, we've complained, and we've looked at a few statistics but not the impact on us. I try to get everyone to think positive. Look to the future. That was my campaign slogan."

"It's valuable to be positive," said Julia. "I can imagine the picture of the town that you all painted last meeting could get voters out. But in terms of getting to a team decision, you're looking for a shift in their thinking. An opening."

"Right. And soon."

"I've found it's a curious thing about change. At some point you need to focus on where you are right now. Kind of a paradox. If you really look closely at your current state, it helps you move toward change more readily."

"You lost me."

Julia nodded. "I know it sounds counter-intuitive. Just think about AA, though. That's a perfect example. Whether you've ever been to a meeting, you've probably seen them on TV or in a movie. What's the first thing people have to say?"

"Hi, I'm Cesar and I'm an alcoholic," he said promptly. "Truth be told, my brother had a problem with alcohol and I went to his meetings when he spoke on his anniversaries of joining."

"Good. So you know. They have to start with where they are. Admitting their alcoholism. Admitting how they've hurt themselves and others. Now let's take that to your meetings. You've spent a lot of time focusing on how you want the mill building to change, right?"

"Sure. So do we talk about how the building looks now? Maybe take a tour?" asked Cesar.

"You could. Although, you've all decided the building is only a piece of the ultimate goal."

"Right. Right! Like a corner of the dance floor. I get it. The bigger goal is to change the town. So does it make sense that we focus on what the town looks like now?" He sat for a minute looking out the window. "Right. Start where we are. Okay." He looked at his watch. "Which is time to go."

"Before we go, I just want to check. Are we good, Cesar?" she asked as she stood up, putting out her hand to him.

Chapter 13

C esar and Julia, and Redley and Mark all ended up walking into the meeting room at the same time. Mark carried a box of donuts, a big thermos of coffee, and a paper bag.

"What's this? All from you?" teased Redley as she helped him set out the coffee and took creamers and sugars out of the bag. She opened the box and said "May I?" and grabbed a sugar-coated cruller without waiting.

"Drug company visit," he said. "But the coffee's on me."

They were standing around the table fixing their coffees and sampling Mark's donuts when Fletcher came rushing in.

"Sorry I'm late," he said, shrugging out of his coat. The rest of them took their seats.

"Not a problem," said Cesar. "Help yourself to some of Mark's goodies here and then we'll get started."

Fletcher poured coffee for himself and sat down, shaking his head to Mark's offer of the donut box.

"We're going to start with a quick check-in," said Cesar, and turned quickly to Julia. "Mine is that I want you all to know that Julia and I had a good talk this morning."

"Did you apologize?" asked Mark quickly. "I hope so."

Cesar laughed. "Figures you'd ask that, Mark. Yes, for your information. We both apologized. We're on the same page and ready to get back to work. She has my full support."

"Wait," said Redley. "I have to ask. Julia, why didn't you defend yourself? You were just trying to help."

Julia hesitated and turned to Cesar. "Shall we take time for this Mayor, or do you want to get started?"

"I had the same question myself," he answered. "So go ahead."

"It's a couple things, really," said Julia. "First of all, you were right, Mayor. I was overzealous. Second of all, and most importantly, when someone is upset, it can makes things worse to challenge them." Julia turned to Redley. "So I chose not to."

"You're making it sound easy. You chose. I can't imagine doing that," answered Redley. "If he spoke to me like that I'd just fight back."

"It takes practice," agreed Julia. "I could have made a choice to argue. If I need to, I do. In this case, if I had, that would have provoked the Mayor to dig in."

"Hey wait," said Cesar. "You're talking about me as if I wasn't in the room."

"You're right," agreed Julia quickly. "You explain what it felt like, Cesar."

"I will. It was like you weren't going to fan the flames," he said. "I knew it immediately. Didn't have to defend myself."

"I think you just did it again, didn't you?" Mark asked Julia, laughing.

"Damn, she did, didn't she?" said Cesar, turning to Mark with surprise.

Julia just smiled. "Defending is a primal response. We all do it."

"But the other day you were just trying to help, do your job. Didn't you get upset? Feel embarrassed, or angry?" asked Redley, her cheeks getting red. "After all, he did it in front of us. Didn't you want to defend yourself? How could you not react?"

"Ouch," said the mayor.

Julia looked thoughtful, as if remembering. "I reacted," she said with a nod. "I've just learned to let it go quickly. I try to heighten my awareness of my reactions. When I notice it, then I have a choice. I can hold on to it or I can get interested and start asking questions. That's what I did."

"So what do you say to yourself at that moment?" asked Mark.

"I ask myself what assumptions am I making. What's going on with this other person? I try to wonder about what they need in that moment."

"What do you mean?" asked Redley, looking from Julia to the mayor. "You were trying to offer him something new to try—a change you thought would help us. Isn't that what he needed?"

"Good question," said Julia. "But you can't force change. The brain is wired to shut down to new ideas when it feels threatened. So when you feel like you have to defend yourself, your brain isn't open to something new, to learning."

"Hmmm," Mark said, as he finished chewing his donut. "So then what?"

Julia shrugged. "Then I have to figure out what's going on with the other person. Maybe the mayor didn't understand. Or maybe he didn't like what I was saying. But it could also be maybe he really doesn't like me or trust me."

"That was it," said Cesar. "At that moment, I wasn't liking what you were doing and I certainly wasn't trusting you."

The others looked uncomfortable but Julia just nodded. "So, in that moment, I couldn't ask you to do something different. *I* had to be the one to do something different. Join you where you were. You were angry with me. How could I argue with that? A feeling is a feeling."

"I'm thinking there's something here I should be paying more attention to," said Mark. "This is what I've got going on at my office with the new software and all. I know we can't take time now, Mayor, but I need to hear more about this."

"You can hire her yourself," said Cesar to Mark. "I can't stop you from that."

"I can send you an article, Mark," said Julia. He gave her his email address, but pressed her until she agreed to stop by the next day for his staff meeting.

"Come on, people. Hasn't this gone on long enough?" Fletcher asked.

"Let's finish the check in," said the mayor, "then I'll explain what we'll focus on this morning. It may surprise you. So, where are you at, Mark?"

"Hmmm. Well, one of our patients finally had her baby yesterday. You know that's the first baby we've delivered this year?"

"Boy or girl?" asked Redley.

"Girl," answered Mark. "Mother and daughter going home tomorrw, doing great. As is my dog, by the way. How about you, Redley?"

"I finally got a national restaurant picking up my Honeymoon Mead."

"Congratulations. Will you have to expand production?" asked the mayor.

Redley nodded. "I was talking about it to one of my distributors and I heard something strange. He asked me whether one of the ideas we were considering was a casino. Can you imagine that?"

Cesar frowned. "You know, I got to believe it's that reporter again. Spreading rumors. I guess I'll have to make time to meet with him. I've been trying to avoid it."

"Well, that's not working," snapped Fletcher. Everyone turned toward him. He shifted in his seat, then picked up his coffee, putting it down again quickly. "I'm just ready to get to work here."

"You haven't checked in," said Redley. "Is everything okay?"

"I don't need to check in," he said, almost sulkily. "Everything's fine."

"Come on," encouraged Redley. "You got the idea of the symphony tuning up."

"So? Even they don't tune up forever. The concert has to start sometime."

Cesar shrugged. "Okay, let's get started."

Cesar described his conversation with Julia that morning. There were some questions about why they should go backward to thinking about where they were now rather than stay focused on the future, but he convinced them to experiment. "Let's just try it."

They spent the next hour reviewing all the issues that plagued the town. The mayor called down to his office to get some data that Fletcher asked for on job loss, per capita income, and population demographics. They explored how it was impacting them each personally.

"It's like I said when we started this morning," said Mark "We hardly ever deliver babies anymore. I've got more patients on Medicare and Medicaid than ever before. People aren't doing anything their insurance won't cover, and some are suffering because of it. Cutting their pills in half. Skipping treatments and visits. It's frustrating to see my practice shift like this. And I used to see everyone around town. In the old stores and restaurants. Now I only see them in my office. It's like they're holed up. What about you, Fletcher? I know it's slower in the branches because I see that myself, but what else?"

Fletcher nodded. "Some of that's the shift to technology but it's worse in this area than others. We've had to go farther and farther afield to find reasonable business loans. I think my loan officers rack up at least double the miles traveling to their customers than they used to. And, obviously, the foreclosures. We now own four of the buildings on Main Street near the mill building because of foreclosures. You know commercial occupancy rates are only about forty percent in town? It's frustrating. Even with favorable terms, there are no potential customers for them. You know we're even considering mobile banking centers just to expand our reach?"

"That's different," said Redley. "What would that mean?"

"Instead of the bricks and mortar and being tied to a vault, it's bringing the bank to the customer. Mostly through technology. It will be hard for some of the staff, I think. What's hard for you Redley? You do so much of your business in other states, now."

"Well, I guess for me," said Redley, "it's the lack of restaurants that hurts us locally the most." She explained how she used to sell to local restaurants and pubs but since so many had gone out of business her sales were mostly wholesale through distributors. She couldn't even consider opening her own restaurant as many breweries do because of the town's economic state. The other problem she talked about was the difficulty convincing good potential employees to move to the area.

"I get tons of applications because people have a romanticized idea of the work," she explained, rolling her eyes. "But then I offer them a job and they check out the area and find out how few young people are around and they turn me down flat."

They were all nodding as they listened to one another. "This is not at all encouraging," said Mark, slumping back in his chair. "I'm getting depressed."

"I'm not," said the mayor. "We've identified a variety of issues that all support our grant application. We needed this data. The grant application will be stronger if we provide not only the numbers but the human stories. Now we've got stories and numbers. You're all touched by this problem. It's not out there. It's in here." He touched his chest. "It's our problem to solve. We can do this. I know we can."

Redley smiled at the gesture, and reached out to pat his hand. "You're not our mayor for nothing, Chief. So what next?"

"We've got a list of town problems we need to solve. Not just what to do with the mill building. Do we all agree?"

Everyone nodded.

"And, we have a list of opportunities we want to create in this town. Right?"

Again they nodded.

"So how about if you each go back and look over your plans and start to match your plan to the gaps we've identified. Project out how your plan would impact each problem. Expand your ideas into a combination business plan and a strategic plan, if you will."

Mark cringed. "I'll try, but you know this isn't my thing."

"How about if I lend you one of my commercial bankers for an afternoon," offered Fletcher. "Marge is probably the best one. She's good."

"That'd be great," said Mark and the mayor at the same time.

"I'm pretty stoked about this. Maybe we can get somewhere," said Redley.

Mark's pager went off. "Damn," he said, looking at it, then looking at his cell phone. He jumped up from his chair. "I need to excuse myself. I've got a major issue going on at the clinic." He rushed out, leaving them wondering what had happened.

Pause and Reflect

Chapter 14

M ark sat in his office looking at the computer. He rolled his shoulders, trying to ease the tension from the day. It had been dark for several hours and he was finishing his patient notes, but his mind was rehashing the day.

He'd received a call from the director of the retirement and nursing complex they attended, with serious complaints about patient care. She listed the shockingly high rate of appointments running late, patients complaining about not being listened to because everyone was looking at the computer screens instead of making eye contact. Mark didn't know how to respond. He had to agree when she pointed to the delay in prescription renewal response with the new system.

He rubbed his eyes and took a deep breath. "I've got to go home," he said to the empty space. "I've got to feed the dog." Then the buzz of an email dropping into his inbox startled him. "Oh, man…" he said. "Who wants me now?" It was the article Julia had promised him. "I'm too tired to read this." He clicked off his computer, put on his leather cap and jacket and took Muldoon out into the chill night air, locking the door behind them.

On the way home, he pressed the music on in his car and flipped to Willie Nelson. He and the dog both enjoyed it.

The next morning when he got to the clinic after his rounds at the hospital, his medical assistant was waiting for him.

"I see you stayed late last night. I think you're the only one close to finishing your charts," she said, handing him a list of patients for the day.

He sighed and scanned it quickly. "Why, what have you heard?"

She shook her head. "Not heard. I just see the piles on the other docs' desks growing higher. They're giving up on the tablets and taking the notes by hand, then leaving them on their desks."

He sighed again. "Well, I've got some help coming today. We're going to have a woman named Julia Breuer at our staff meeting."

When she reminded him he had cancelled the meeting because everyone had said they didn't need any more instruction, his face reddened and she quickly ducked out the door.

He looked at his watch and then at the list of patients. He didn't have time to call Julia and tell her to reschedule. He figured he could call her at ten when he had an open slot. Of course, when ten came he was backed up and the slot was filled, then suddenly it was noon and Julia had arrived in the waiting room. He grabbed his leather jacket and took her arm.

"Come on. I'll take you for a quick lunch at the diner."

"I thought I was here to watch a meeting?" she asked.

He explained as they walked across the street. "Perhaps I can just tell you what's going on and you can suggest something."

The interior of the diner was old metal and faded red leatherette. It looked sadly neglected. They sat down in a booth and ordered a tuna salad for her and a fried egg sandwich for him. The waitress brought them each a thick white mug full of steaming coffee.

"Look," said Mark, "Let me explain." He told her about constant shifts in healthcare regulations requiring them to change their office practices for maintaining patient information. They had to start with electronic medical records or EMR's, then add connectivity to other systems.

"We never really got on board with the EMR's before we had to get into the newer system. That's been over eighteen months in development," said Mark, squinting with worry, "and we're behind. I worked on it with my office manager endlessly. We had to have the right match of forms, information flow, fields, and communication potential for our needs and patient population."

He slumped back again against the torn upholstery of the bench seat. "Damn, that whole thing was incredibly painful. I'm not a techie. I will say one thing. I know a whole lot more than I used to. My manager kept me at it, thankfully. We had to get it done, you know? The regulators, and now the insurance companies, are requiring compliance. This is only one issue. With all the changes going on in healthcare, it's inevitable that we'll have more to come."

Julia just nodded, sipped her coffee, and waited. There were a few people coming in for lunch, most taking a stool at the counter across the aisle from them.

"I was sure we'd thought of everything," Mark went on. "Four months ago everything was installed, the software vendor came in and gave everyone instruction. We went live with the system three months ago. It should have been fine!" Mark grimaced and slumped against the booth.

"I take it you're not fine?" asked Julia.

"No! Far from it. I expected a few glitches. I had no clue they'd abandon it before they even got started. They were complaining from the first day."

"Not surprising with a change that big," said Julia.

Mark looked up. "Really?" He sighed. "They complained about the screen layouts, about the time everything took. They complained about the training. I was sympathetic at first. Just told them to go slow and they'd get it. But they kept complaining. They aren't complaining as much now, but they're not using it. Because the records aren't in the system, none of the bills are going out. There are other issues with prescriptions. It's a nightmare. I don't get what their issue is."

"I see that you don't," said Julia. "That's often part of the problem in many change efforts. The leader is out in front and can't figure out why the staff isn't following."

"Exactly!" exclaimed Mark. "You see this in other changes? I'm not alone?"

"Of course not," said Julia, reassuring him. "So here's the thing, Mark. First of all, you were involved in that project for how many months before the rest of your team?"

At that moment, the waitress delivered their sandwiches on turquoise plastic plates heaping with fries. She grabbed ketchup from the next booth and set it on their table. "You folks all set?"

Mark nodded, and then turned back to focus on Julia. "I started that project months and months ago." He peeled open his sandwich and shook ketchup onto it. "Over a year before we rolled it out, I guess."

"Okay, so first of all, you've got a year's more experience with it than they do."

"But I just started using it same time they did," Mark objected.

Julia shook her head. "Not what I mean. You started out feeling the pain of the problems—those insurance and regulatory issues you mentioned. You explored lots of different possible solutions, right? You probably met with a number of different vendors, reviewed proposals, or something like that."

Mark nodded. "We saw five different samples of EMR systems the first time alone."

"Exactly. And you picked the one you did for a reason, getting very familiar with it during the process of determining the pros and cons of each."

Mark nodded again, and took a bite of his sandwich.

"Then you worked on customizing it for your clinic," said Julia. "I'm saying that it became part of your thinking about the way you care for a patient *way* before the rest of your office. When you went live, you just had to learn the software, you didn't have to readjust your whole mindset."

Mark sat up straight. "You're right. Completely right. It's been so long I'd forgotten how annoyed I was, and worried about how it was going to get in my way."

"You're like lots of leaders," said Julia. "There's a cycle of steps you go through in successful change, whether it's personal change like buying a new house, or organizational change similar to what you're going through."

"What do you mean?" he asked.

"Let's say a young couple wants to buy a house, but needs their parents to co-sign. They look at lots of houses and then bring their parents right to the one they love. Their parents can't say yes because they're just at the first step of understanding the market and have no frame of reference."

"That happened to me, but opposite," said Mark. "It was my parents who were looking but I was going to own it. They showed me just one house and I resisted okaying it at first, until I shopped around a bit online."

Julia went on. "So you know what it feels like to come in late. In an organizational change, the leader gets way out ahead, whether it's one person or the senior leadership team, or maybe the project team in charge of the initiative. They become aware of the problem, engaging with one another or with experts to talk about it, and figure out potential solutions. They develop a plan. Then they move into action—in your case purchasing the system and having it installed. Everyone else in the organization is still at square one."

Mark sighed and picked up a French fry. "It's good to know I'm not the only stupid one."

"Clearly, stupidity is not your issue, Mark. It's understanding change as a process that's new for you."

"They didn't teach that in med school."

"Most of us learn it the hard way, unfortunately," agreed Julia. "It ought to be taught to us as kids, you know? It could be taught in the Boy Scouts or Girl Scouts, maybe. Think about them learning that if you're on a hike and you're the leader, you can't get way out in front of the rest of the group."

"You know, that's really true. I went on an Appalachian Mountain Club hike and the guide was the only one who knew the trail. He was careful to keep us together, and it wasn't easy with some young kids running ahead and us old fogies bringing up the rear."

"So, right now you're the hiking guide and you've been striding out front, with the only map. You're already crossing over the top of the mountain, but your team has barely moved from where you all started."

Chapter 15

"**I**f I'm the leader and I'm way out front, now what?" asked Mark. "I think I'm hearing you saying I should have involved them all along. But what can I do?"

"Certainly, it might have helped to involve them more in planning your medical record change, but that's in the past," said Julia. "Right now they're still near the parking lot of the hike. In a way, you do have to go back to where they are."

Mark looked over at the counter where a couple was sitting on adjacent stools, their empty plates pushed aside as they shared a newspaper between them. "Should I share all the proposals?"

"I'm thinking more about the comment you made earlier. How worried you were about how it would change the way you worked with patients."

"Right." Mark had finished his sandwich and reached over to fiddle with the one of the mini juke boxes that was installed in each booth. "These used to be the way we listened to music. When I travel I see iPads mounted in the new diner booths. I imagine some people need help using them. Things have changed so much."

"Have you talked with your people about their concerns about the change? Asked them questions? Listened to their issues?"

"Just a bit at first. Basically, I thought they just didn't understand. I brought the software vendor back for extra training."

"Did that help?"

"A couple people. The rest just wanted to convince me to go back to the old way," said Mark.

"We tend to hold on to the old when the new feels uncomfortable, or fearful," said Julia. "I think there's also something about the old brain patterns that get reinforced and make it easy to keep doing something the same way, but you'd know more about it than I."

Mark nodded. "You know, I feel that way myself. Sometimes it feels like the whole practice I learned of working with my patients is being threatened. By malpractice insurance. By insurance companies. By regulations. I know there's only more change coming we'll all have to get used to."

"So is that true for your staff in this situation?"

"Sure. Specifically in this case, I know some of the older ones first said they don't like computers in the exam rooms. This system has robust analytical tools. It may be that some of them are worried that I'll have more data to check up on them, but they haven't said it out loud."

"So you were lucky they were complaining to you," said Julia. "Stuff is easier to manage when it's out in the open. It's probably worse now that they're quiet."

"Oh great. So somehow I've made things worse?" moaned Mark. The waitress came by and asked if they wanted dessert. Mark ordered a piece of the apple pie displayed under a glass dome on the counter across from them.

"Nothing for me, thanks," said Julia, waiting to continue until the waitress cleared the table and brought Mark his pie.

"Resistance to change was likely no matter what. Now you just need to get curious about what they're feeling and deal with it."

"How? That's what I don't know."

"You have to figure out what's going on for people. Just like you said, it may be different for each person," explained Julia. "For a few, it may simply be a matter of more training. They just don't get how to do it. They may not get the software, or they may not understand why it's important to your practice. Either way those folks just need more information."

"That's what I thought I was doing," complained Mark.

"Yes, but more often it's emotion that gets in the way—the old elephant in the room. You said some don't like computers in the exam rooms. You'll have to get them to talk about it. Why they don't like it? I would think for those who aren't quick on a keyboard, it is time consuming, right? More time than writing by hand?"

Mark nodded. "True. My staff is dedicated to good patient care. They want to keep good records. That's why some of them are complaining. The old system was pretty quick. They think this new one gets in the way of good care."

"So, they don't like it because it gets in the way of their patient care. Are they right?" asked Julia. "If so, first they need to talk about it. Then strategize. Maybe there's some voice recognition software or typing lessons or drop down menus that could help them. Rearrange the rooms—that's the environmental solution. Maybe you will have to hire staff to take care of it. I don't know, but you need to know. Listen to them. You might even find out that there are some real problems with the system itself that could be improved."

"Okay. I get it. People each respond to change in different ways depending on what's going on for them."

"Exactly. I can't tell from what you're saying, but sometimes they may not buy into change because they don't trust you. Remember the mayor and I talking about that?"

Mark put his chin on his hands and frowned. He was quiet for a bit and Julia didn't interrupt his thinking.

"I don't think I have that problem," he said slowly. "But I'll have to think about it. When my office manager was around I didn't have that much contact with the front office staff. I think the medical staff trusts me, but I'm not sure the newer office folks do. I hardly know some of them."

"Would that be something to work on?" asked Julia.

"How? They've all been here a long time. It would seem weird to go introduce myself, don't you think?"

Julia shook her head. "You know how to make connections. You care about people. You just have to make the clerical staff a priority. Just like you would a patient. All of this is about building followership. That's your job as a leader. To inspire people to want to do what's necessary. Get them to follow you. Inspire them."

"Seems like I've got a lot to do." He pulled out his wallet and left some bills on the table with the check.

"I'm going to leave you to it, then," said Julia, sliding out of her booth and putting her jacket on.

Mark walked out with her and leaned over, giving her an awkward quick hug. "Thank you, Julia. You asked some hard questions, but you're a good listener. It felt good to talk about it. Gave me quite a bit to think about. Perhaps too much."

"So, just take one thing and put it to use. What one thing will you pay attention to today?" asked Julia.

"Who doesn't understand, who doesn't like it, and who the heck do I hardly know?"

Chapter 16

The next time Julia and Mark saw each other was at the Blue Ribbon Committee meeting. Mark was thanking her for her help when Fletcher walked into the conference room.

"I haven't gotten too far with it yet, but I'm seeing things differently," finished Mark. "So thank you." He turned to Fletcher. "And I owe thanks to you, too, Fletcher. I couldn't have gotten this plan together without the help from Marge. I'm excited about what we put together." He patted the file folder on the table in front of him.

"She was, too," said Fletcher. "Apparently you did some good work together."

"Oh, did she show you already?" asked Mark, sounding disappointed.

"No. She said she'd leave that to you."

Redley walked in, and dropped a thick blue folder on the table. "I hope we get somewhere today. That took a lot of work. How'd you do, Mark?"

"Surprisingly well. Marge taught me about business plans. I've been learning a lot this week. I had Julia teaching me about being more of a leader, building... what was the word you used at the end of lunch, Julia? Followership?"

"Followership?" said Redley, wrinkling her nose. "What an awful word. I hate the word follower. It makes me think of people who've been brainwashed. You know, the living dead?"

"What are you talking about," said Fletcher, rather too loudly. Redley and Mark both looked startled and Fletcher apologized quickly. "Sorry, but good business, good society in fact, is based on leaders and followers. If there were no followers, who'd get all the work done?"

"Good grief," said Redley. "That's archaic. I have a flat organization. People work very independently. It's not about leaders and followers. I try to teach people what to do so everyone's a leader."

"That can't work. Someone has to make the decisions," said Fletcher. "Someone has higher accountability. You have to have a hierarchy."

"No, you don't!" argued Redley, red creeping from her neck to her face. "That's such a typical banking term. You probably have an organization chart cast in stone with lots of arrows and lines and all. You've got your Executive VPs and your Senior VPs and then your VPs and your…"

"STOP!" said Mark loudly. He stood up. "That's enough. You're doing exactly what Julia has taught us not to do." He sat back down a little sheepishly. "Now, since I said the word followership, someone get curious about what I meant."

Redley suddenly laughed, breaking the tense moment. "You go, Mark! What's followership?"

"Yes," said Fletcher. "Tell us what you meant by followership."

"I'm not sure I'm the best one to answer and I'll defer to Julia in a minute," said Mark. "But, here's what I meant. Getting people to understand an idea. Getting them to buy into it. To be inspired. To want to go along."

"Sounds like a cult," said Fletcher, but he actually smiled a little.

Mark turned to his left. "What about it, Julia? Did I say what you meant?"

"Sure. That's part of it. As a leader you can't just tell people what to do. Sure, sometimes you have to, but that runs thin pretty quickly. Just think of a two year old to know how much being in charge doesn't give you all the power. Right?"

"Exactly," said Mark. "So you have to get people to understand why, to know what to do, and to be inspired to do it. Not so easy."

"But what about who's ultimately responsible?" asked Fletcher.

"Important question," said Julia. "There is accountability that comes with leadership. Some people have higher levels of it than others. You, Redley, have the highest level of accountability in your firm since you own it, right?"

Redley nodded. "But I like to think that we're pretty flat at my place, and sometimes I might be the follower."

Julia agreed. "Leadership and followership can shift under different circumstances. You can even have informal leaders. I watched some of my teams have leaders that developed that weren't the team captains. Leadership is about influence, not just titles or roles. Sometimes for the good. Occasionally not so good."

"But someone always has to be in charge," asserted Fletcher.

"In a formal organization, there is a leader, or group of leaders in charge," agreed Julia. "But some self-organizing groups have no designated leader. Like many book groups. Or AA. That's a large example. The Internet, if you want to get to a really large system."

The door flew open and the mayor rushed in, his briefcase in hand. "You're all here. Sorry I'm late. That damned reporter. He's been calling all my staff. Everyone came to me to tell me how they couldn't get rid of him."

They waited while the mayor took off his coat and settled himself in a chair, all the while talking about his conversations with his staff about the reporter. "Asked all kinds of questions about our committee. He said the town's complaining about our secrecy. Why we haven't gotten more done. When a decision would be announced. How much we're paying Julia. Then he really went crazy."

"What does that mean?" asked Redley. "Did he threaten them or something?"

"No, but crazy ideas. Asked if we had considered an indoor roller coaster, do you believe it? And a casino. He asked everyone about whether we had decided to open a casino. Said he had heard they would create jobs and bring in needed tax revenue. I knew it was him that was starting that rumor you heard, Redley."

"Mayor," said Fletcher slowly. "I think we have a problem. I heard something about a casino, too. At the state bankers meeting. I squashed it immediately, of course. Now I'm thinking somehow we've gotten some bad PR out there."

"Wait a minute," said Redley. "What if it isn't bad PR or the reporter? What if there really is a casino operator out there sniffing around the mill building. I mean, if we don't get the grant, that building will be empty and available. Our Purchase and Sale is null and void if we don't get the grant. What if there's some investor out there considering turning it into a casino? Wouldn't that be a good thing?"

The mayor slammed his fist on the table. "I won't have a damn casino in my town. Not on my watch! Never!"

Chapter 17

R edley was the first to break the silence. "Do I take it this is personal, Chief?"

"Look here, I had a buddy, a close buddy in the service, who was a gambling addict. I saw what it did to him and his family," said Cesar. "I don't want that happening in this town. That's it."

"But they have help for people like that now. We have to keep an open mind. I'm not sure a casino would be all that bad," said Redley, finishing her sentence in spite of the glares directed at her from around the table. "It's better than an empty building. We should find out more about who might be interested. Whether they're credible. Maybe we might join forces if we can't get the grant."

"Not bad for you and your bottom line," said Fletcher. "You can sell lots of your beer and mead to them. A great new client. In fact you probably would encourage the idea."

"Give me a break, Fletcher," said Redley, almost out of her chair. "That's not what I meant!"

"Crime might go up," said Cesar. "Certainly need to increase the size of our police force. We don't have the funds for that."

"A casino wouldn't bring families in," moaned Mark. "They'd all be transient. Traveling in on buses for day trips. Not settling here. I can't imagine anyone else in town would like this. We've got to get the word out to our local families to squash this idea."

"You can bet that my bank wouldn't be seeing a dime of any of that casino money," said Fletcher. "And they'd force some of the few local restaurants out of ..."

"Can't be a good influence on the kids in town," interrupted Mark.

"Oh no," went on Fletcher, "they'd have some big city commercial bank full of investment bankers that get huge bonuses managing their accounts. Not the local bank, no matter how good we are. We need to put a stop to this!"

"Maybe this is just a plant by that reporter to discredit my committee," wondered Cesar, not really addressing anyone. "He was always after me. A casino wouldn't want to open here. We don't have the right population base for it. I just can't see it."

"Come on, people. You have to think about the potential income to the town," said Redley.

The mayor interrupted, speaking louder when she kept talking. "All the recent evidence in the municipal press and tax reviews says that the casinos already out there aren't making the promised money for the towns or the states they're in. Plus, we'd have water problems, sewer problems. I don't like it for our town. I need to get to that reporter. Maybe we should put out a press release about our progress."

"May I say something?" asked Julia.

They all turned to her with a similar expression of surprise, as if they'd forgotten she was even there.

"Don't tell me we're doing something well?" Cesar asked.

"Actually, you are shifting back to your behavior from the first meeting I came to. You are clearly stating your opinions. One after the other."

They looked from one to another, and back to Julia.

"No questions," said Mark. "Right?"

Julia shrugged. "Stress can throw you back to default behavior and then it's easy to forget anything new," she added. "Whether financial pressures, or time pressures, or any other reason—like the news you think you have."

"The news we *think* we have?" asked Cesar, scowling.

"Wait. Hear me out," said Julia calmly. "You don't know what's truly going on. You have a few pieces of data that you've put together and come to different possible conclusions. Not surprising. Each person organizes data differently from your own perspectives. You've created a picture from the pieces, and each of you have created a different picture."

They looked at one another.

"And since you're all leaders, you're ready to jump into action. That's what leaders do. They see a problem and they rush to solve it."

"So what should I do, as leader?" asked Cesar, pushing himself out of his chair and pacing across the room. "Don't I need to jump into action?"

"At some point, maybe. Now, maybe not. You might want to first encourage the group to slow down," said Julia, her own voice slowing and softening. She waited in silence until the mayor came back to the table and settled into his chair.

"Remember, you're a team," she said. "With my field hockey teams, when we encountered an unusually good player that was racking up points for the other team, often everyone got panicked." She stopped and made eye contact with each of them. "They would want to take their own individual action to stop the momentum and they'd forget the game plan. Does that make sense to you?" She waited for assent.

"Yeah," admitted Redley. "That seems pretty accurate. I guess we were all going off in our own directions?"

"Good description," said Julia. "Think about birds. Think how effectively they move as a flock, swooping through the air together. Now imagine a hawk flying into their midst. Danger. What do they do?"

"They scatter," answered Redley. "I saw it out my window a few times when we first moved into the building. The flocks over the river just scattered."

"Exactly. They all do their own thing and break their connection with one another. Quickly, though, a flock of birds comes back together on their own."

"So what did you do with your teams to bring them back together?" asked Cesar.

"I'd call a time out and get them to pay attention to each other. To slow down and increase their awareness of each other and our game plan. To remember how they could join in defeating the opponent, as a team."

"That's what you're trying to do now, aren't you, Julia?" asked Cesar.

She nodded.

Fletcher tapped the folder in front of him with his glasses. "We came in here with our expanded strategic plans to share and we aren't even talking about them."

"Right," said the mayor. "That casino thing threw me. It was a shock."

Fletcher and Mark both nodded.

Cesar looked at Julia and when she didn't say anything he took a deep breath and let it out slowly. "How about this? Let's slow down. Review each plan. Ask each other questions to really flesh them out. Then what? Someone help me. I'm still so annoyed I can't think straight."

Chapter 18

"**Y**ou asked for us to help you?" asked Redley. "I'm impressed."

"Why?" asked Cesar. "I'm not impressive when I can't think what to do next."

"On the contrary," said Julia. "Redley's right to be impressed. What you just did is a high level leadership skill. Demonstrating vulnerability by saying you're stuck. Sharing leadership. You're also showing your respect for the skills of the rest of your team by relying on them."

Cesar just shifted in his chair uncomfortably.

"So what do we do, you asked? Maybe counter any bad rumors with our own PR," answered Redley. "We need some good PR."

"I'm not the business person, but it seems to me we've been too quiet about our work. We need to connect the committee with the rest of the community somehow," said Mark. He turned quickly to look at Julia. "I hadn't noticed the parallel until I said it out loud. This is what we were talking about with the process of change the other day, right? We're out in front of the town thinking about this."

"What are you talking about?" asked Fletcher. "Out in front?"

"Remember I said Julia came to my office and we talked about change and followership?"

Fletcher nodded.

"She helped me see I'm going about things all wrong with this switch over of electronic records. This is the same thing," explained Mark.

"I don't get it," said Fletcher.

"It's like we're hiking up the mountain and leaving the whole town at the base camp," said Mark, pointing up in the air with one hand and down at the ground with the other.

"You really aren't making any sense, Mark," said the mayor.

"Julia, help," asked Mark. "I'm doing it again. Jumping ahead and skipping steps in my explanation so they don't get it."

Julia explained what she'd told Mark about leaders often being way out ahead of their organization on change projects. Having identified the problem, considered potential solutions, and made an informed choice, they roll out the change. Then they don't understand why everyone doesn't immediately join in the parade.

"Right," said Mark, joining in. "Like she said, we've been here meeting month after month. We've walked the building, considered alternatives, explored how we'd like to see the town in the future and what the problems are in town now. We've each proposed ideas we've spent a fair amount of time developing."

"Exactly what we should be doing," said Fletcher. "What are you suggesting we do now? I don't see where you're going."

"The town! The rest of the town! We need to get them involved."

"Wait a minute," said Redley. "You're saying instead of PR about what we're doing, we go out and actually involve them?"

"Yes," said Mark, nodding his head emphatically. "In some way. We shouldn't do this alone. I'm getting that now. What do you all think? Do you see what I mean?"

"I think I do. I like it," said Cesar slowly, also nodding his head. "I like it a lot. We could go out there and do some sort of info sessions. Some sort of community meetings. This could be great. We'd shut that reporter right up about our secrecy and our not doing anything."

"Actually, Chief," said Redley, "do you think maybe it would be the reverse? Wouldn't we be giving him lots to talk about?"

Cesar grinned. "We would. All good stuff. I like it!" he repeated. "What do you think, Julia?"

"I'm noticing that people are asking real questions, considering answers, weighing in. Has everyone voiced an opinion?" she asked gently.

"No," said Cesar, after a brief pause. He swiveled his chair around. "Fletcher, we haven't heard from you. What do you think? We need to all be in agreement on this. Is it a good idea or do you see problems?"

Fletcher sat with his elbows on the table and his fingertips touching. "I'm not sure. It could be risky. We'd be showing our hand pretty early. We might spend a lot of time fielding complaints or even lots of crank ideas we would never want to invest in."

"Well, that's a good point," said the mayor. "That's why we need different opinions on this. Makes sense that a banker would think about risk."

"Still," went on Fletcher, "I do get what Mark is trying to say, you know, about us getting out in front of everyone."

"Really?" asked Mark.

"I've had that happen at the bank when a new product gets rolled out. The development team's all excited because they've been working for months on it, and the customer service folks see it in it's final stage and say why on earth do we need this?"

"That happens even at your bank?" asked Mark, sounding incredulous. "With all your systems and checks and balances?"

"Sure. More than once," said Fletcher, half laughing at Mark's disbelief. "I don't like the idea of these rumors flying around. Better to get something good out there for people to talk about. Otherwise they make up their own stories."

"So are we in agreement?" asked Cesar. Everyone nodded. "All right, let's get to the details of each plan. Who wants to go first?"

Fletcher looked at his watch. "I'm not sure we'll have time for all of them today. I have a hard stop in thirty minutes."

"Me, too," said Mark. "I have a team meeting at the clinic."

"Okay," said Cesar. "Let's take a few minutes to review where we are and next steps."

"Should we have a referendum?" asked Mark.

They discussed it, but finally Cesar said they didn't have time or money for that. Redley came up with the idea of a survey. "I remember you did a little survey of your customers, Fletcher. We could just do it online for the whole town. We can get public input for free that way. It's immediate. I'll contribute the time to create it—I've got a great social media person on my marketing team."

Fletcher sighed.

"What's wrong?" asked Redley.

"Nothing. I just can't figure out this social media stuff. Never mind," he said, shaking his head. "Not important. It's just that my son is so into Facebook and Hulu or Zulu or whatever. Never mind."

"So how do you all feel about where we are?" asked the mayor.

"I like it," said Redley. "I'd like us to schedule an extra meeting to share our plans. We need to do it quickly because it will inform the survey."

"Right," said the mayor.

"I like that we're including the community," said Mark. "Could we get together for a dinner meeting instead of these morning meetings to present our plans? That way we'd have more time."

Redley nodded. "I'll supply beverages."

"I'd be willing," said Fletcher.

"How about the community online survey," asked the mayor. "How do you feel about that, Fletcher?"

"I'm good. As long as I don't have to manage it. We should think of a way to get opinions of people who don't have computers, though."

"How about something at the town hall?" asked Mark. "Or libraries?"

Cesar nodded. "I'll have my staff figure something out. Good idea. We're almost out of time." He turned purposefully. "What do you think, Julia?"

She nodded. "Let me ask you, Cesar."

He nodded and looked around the table. "I'd say we recovered pretty well. Everyone spoke to their opinion. We've verified next steps. I'd say we're good."

They made arrangements for a dinner meeting and adjourned.

"Walk with me back to my office, will you Julia?" asked Cesar.

Pause and Reflect

Chapter 19

It wasn't sunny but the clouds were brightening as Cesar and Julia walked past the lobby windows of the town hall.

"That ended up a good meeting, Julia, don't you think? You caught that I'd left out Fletcher from the decision about going public. I missed that."

"It's easy to get caught up in content. You brought him out more thoroughly at the end."

"I was paying attention that time. How do I remember, though?" asked Cesar. "I tend to let the momentum take me and sometimes I forget people or run over them."

"What I try to do is to scan the faces at the table from time to time. Just look from one to the other. Especially when making a decision. Then, it's really important to scan the room. I look at their expressions and their body language. Sometimes people nod yes but their face or their body is saying no."

"People give a lot away, don't they, if you're aware enough to watch for it?"

"Most of us, do. Except the women with Botox and the men who play poker," she said with a grin.

"So, I pay attention to their faces and body language."

"Remembering to just look around the table is an easy first step. Sounds simple but it becomes a sort of cue. It's kind of like activating a personal radar system."

"Women are better at that," said Cesar, "like my wife is."

"Wait a minute, didn't you have to do it as a police officer?" asked Julia, as they reached the door to his office. "And becoming mayor. You had to read people when you were campaigning, right?"

Cesar shrugged and put up his hands. "Somehow I have these skills I'm not making use of. Seems like a waste. I'm learning though. I really feel like we're making progress. Don't you think? There's a lot of forward momentum."

Julia nodded. "You've mobilized."

"What do you mean?"

"It's a stage of how work gets done. Planning, data gathering."

Cesar looked at his watch. "Tell me next time, Julia. I've got to run." He grinned. "Plus, there are only so many lectures I can take in a day."

"I'm so glad you're honest with me," Julia said, grinning back at him. "It makes it so much easier to work with you."

Chapter 20

They sat around the mayor's conference table surrounded by open boxes of pizza and bottles of Red Tankard Ale. The tall windows overlooking Main Street were dark except for the reflected glow of one neon sign in a shop window. They were finishing checking in.

"You're pretty quiet tonight," said Mark to Fletcher. "Everything okay?"

"Oh, you know. People problems. Angie again."

"Has she finally walked out on you?" asked Redley with a laugh, but then quieted at the hurt expression on Fletcher's face.

"Never mind," said Fletcher quickly. "Let's get to work."

"Wait a minute. You brought it up. What about Angie?" asked Cesar.

Fletcher shook his head. "Things were going better, and now they're worse."

"What's wrong?" asked Redley.

"Every time I see her now I'm just trying to figure out what she wants," said Fletcher, wiping his hands on a napkin. "I feel so awkward. I complimented her yesterday afternoon. She's on this project team to raise money for the United Way. I said how great she's doing in front of the whole team and she just turned red and got silent. I don't get it."

"Maybe she just wants to be appreciated, Fletcher," said Cesar.

"That's what I was doing, wasn't I?" he snapped. "Wasn't I?" Fletcher had turned to Julia.

"You know," said Julia, "sometimes it makes people uncomfortable to be singled out."

"I just want to say I'm impressed you're trying, Fletcher," said Redley.

"It's not helping," he said, looking discouraged.

"Maybe not yet, but it will," said Julia. "You'll get better at this now that you're paying attention."

"I'm not getting better," complained Fletcher, tapping his fingers against his coffee cup.

"You noticed that she turned red and got silent. Would you have noticed that before?" asked Julia.

"Never!" said Redley, then apologized quickly.

"She's right. I wouldn't have," admitted Fletcher.

"So you're starting to get better at paying attention to the impact of your action," said Julia.

"I guess I am," said Fletcher, a bit of surprised pleasure in his voice. "But what did I do wrong?"

"Okay. So you praised her," answered Julia. "But when you single someone out of a group like that, you are separating the group. Some people don't like that."

"Like teacher's pet?" asked Mark.

"Exactly," said Julia.

Fletcher looked thoughtful. "So it would have probably been okay had I done it afterward in private?"

Julia nodded.

He sighed. "I think it was easier before I was aware. I didn't have so many choices." They all laughed. "Okay, let's get to work," said Fletcher.

Chapter 21

"Who's first?" asked Cesar.

Redley raised her hand quickly. "I will. I have a pro forma here and copies for each of you." She passed around the papers.

"I have data on the costs of rehabbing the building into small offices that can be flexed up or down as the start-up businesses grow and need more space. Or if they get too big and move to their own space, we can shrink down and bring in new start-ups. I'm including a big common area where people can come together and share ideas. Cross-fertilization, so to speak. A creative bull pen. I've got research that shows that creativity is sparked that way."

"What do you mean?" asked Cesar.

"There was this old ark of a building at MIT that had scientists from different disciplines who didn't have office space anywhere else. The offices were numbered strangely and they were all mixed together. It was an amazingly fertile space for scientific discoveries and even business ventures. The company Bose came out of there. Getting people physically together is part of the importance of an incubator, according to what I've found of best practices."

"Could that be accessible to the public?" asked Mark.

"I hadn't thought about that," said Redley. "Why not? That's a great idea. It could be partly public meeting space. Then the start-ups could also use it to make community presentations. Maybe do some stuff with the local high school and the tech school. I like that, Mark."

"How about a coffee shop in there?" offered Cesar.

"Another great idea. I read that when Steve Jobs designed the space for Pixar studios, he put the coffee shop, cafeteria, mailboxes, and even the bathrooms all in a common area in the lobby so people would have to mix." She paused and looked around the table.

"This is good, Redley. What else?" encouraged Cesar.

"I also thought we could have ground floor office space for rent for local professionals. Some incubators are really a contest. There's one that gets something like twelve hundred applications for each spot."

"You're kidding," said Fletcher. "Where do they all come from?"

"Around the world. That program is really well known."

"What's the appeal?" Fletcher probed.

"Those that get selected each session are provided a rigorous training and support program to make sure they are viable. Then, hopefully the angel investors are waiting in the wings to help launch the companies. Obviously, that's the appeal. The angel investors like it because the businesses are already vetted, and the appeal to the start-ups is obvious."

"I had no idea," said Cesar.

"Me either," said Fletcher.

"In my budget, the professionals providing that close mentoring would be paid from our grant money for the first five years and then we could find another source of funding. Potentially angel investors. Start-ups need legal advice, financial advice, patent advice, all kinds of professional services. We will have to put together an intense mentoring program that practically guarantees success. They need good ideas but they need good skills. We won't start out with twelve hundred applicants, but we might want to make it competitive. I think we'd want to require them to grow locally for some period of time."

"We might be able to do something collaboratively with the EDBA," said Fletcher.

"EDBA?" asked Mark.

"Economic Development and Business Administration. It's a state program. They have a variety of funding for education and support for small businesses. It's a very new program designed to develop new jobs."

"This is great, guys," said Redley. "When we talked about the town needs, we talked about how to get young people and jobs for them. Small business growth is one great way, right?"

"Nationally, small businesses are a huge source of new job growth," explained Fletcher.

"This is really personal to me," said Redley, picking up one of the beer bottles and looking at it in her hand. "I had such a hard time starting my business. I couldn't get the time of day from anyone at first. I mean, it was hard enough to start a business in that economy ten years ago. Then, there were all the details, the learning curve was so steep. Plus, I kept running into such skepticism about the possibilities of success, and difficulty getting funding, particularly because I was a woman."

Fletcher shifted in his chair. "Now Redley…"

"No wait, Fletcher. Let me finish. Do you know at that time there were around fourteen hundred micro breweries in the country and only about sixty women in leadership roles in the business? In the whole country!!! The whole country! Since that time there's been a three thousand percent growth in the business, but hardly any more women involved. I had a hard time being taken seriously. In spite of my training and early success out of my basement. By distributors. By vendors. By banks, although I must admit when I finally got to yours, Fletcher, I'd had some minor success and your guys were willing to take a chance. But, I'd go to a tasting event and people would look right by me to talk to my assistant, who was a man. But, that's beside the point. It's just that I made it and I want other businesses to make it, too. Especially in this town."

"We're all glad you did," said the mayor. "Particularly buying the foreclosed theatre. I'm so glad you didn't tear the building down."

Redley grinned. "I know you are," she said with a mischievous expression. "Look. I want other want-to-be entrepreneurs, and let's face it, including and maybe especially the women, to have an easier time. But, I really think this would be good for the town. Really good for the town."

Fletcher and Mark both nodded slowly, thoughtfully.

"This is off topic, but what made you choose such a hard business for women to enter anyway?" asked Mark.

"And, why a business that takes so much capital?" asked Fletcher. "You have a lot of equipment involved. Fixed costs, etc."

"I didn't really choose it. It just sort of happened. I wasn't much of a success in school at first. What I loved was going to music concerts and festivals. I'd make all these specialty lemonades to sell at them so I could make the money back for the tickets. I was using honey to flavor them. I got really interested in all the different honeys. Then I discovered mead, which is basically fermented honey and water. It was really simple to make—you take honey and water and just add yeast. I started to make it in my basement. I was hooked. Went to school at UC Davis. They're known for their wine program, but I fell in love with the beer lab. The rest, as they say, is history."

"Wait," asked Fletcher. "I don't remember you coming to our bank for loans until you did that first expansion. Where did you get your initial funding?"

"My mother and a few friends. That's why I came back to the East Coast. I had sold shares one at a time to individuals, but still didn't have enough money for the start up costs. She mortgaged her house to get me the final lump sum," said Redley quietly. "What a responsibility to carry! She took out the loan with a mortgage company, not a bank, at the height of the market when they weren't asking many questions and didn't require income certification. Then when the market dropped the loan was a lot higher than the value of the house. I was struggling big time. I couldn't make the payments and she certainly couldn't. She lives on a very small teacher's pension. She couldn't sell it. It went to the beginning stages of foreclosure."

"Wow," said Mark. "That must have put some extreme pressure on you!"

Redley nodded and took a swig of beer. "Only two things saved us. When the financial crisis caused all that hoopla about subprime mortgages and predatory lending, there was a time when they were re-setting loans. It was also at the turning point of my business. We started to turn a profit. So, I had enough money to make the new payments. My mother kept her house. We survived. It sure wasn't easy. Gradually, I paid off the mortgage and I've paid back all of the initial investors. So ever since, my goal has been to support other new businesses. I was thinking I could start an internship program at the brewery and affiliate it with the business incubator program."

"What about the university?" asked Cesar. "I thought you said a few meetings ago there was some possibilities with them."

"Absolutely. I talked with the dean of the business school last Tuesday. It's pretty amazing news. He's always liked the idea but he was able to share something big. He said they got a huge private grant for a new Center for Entrepreneurial Studies. They'll tie it to their biotech engineering program as well as their business school. It's been in the works for a while but they are just getting ready to make the formal press release. They would love to talk about affiliating with us if it gets to that point."

Redley finished reviewing her pro forma with lots of questions and ideas from the others. Then it was Mark's turn.

Pause and Reflect

Chapter 22

"This is the first time I've made a financial presentation, but I know you guys will help me." He handed around his set of papers and also had one for Julia.

"Since Redley explained both the rational reasons for her plan and the personal ones, I thought I'd do the same. Fletcher, you know some of the story, but I'd like Redley and Julia to hear it too. You may know some of it, Mayor, but I think you were off on active duty for several of the years, so some of this may be new to you, too."

Mark looked around the table and took a deep breath. Cesar's cell phone vibrated on the table. He looked at it, then pressed a button that stopped the vibrating and turned toward Mark.

"I don't often talk about my personal life," said Mark. "I figure it's no one's business but mine. I hear a lot of stories from my patients and, well, I'm… I'm the healthy one, need to have the answers, I don't know, … powerful. I'm supposed to be able to fix everything, at least that's what they think."

Julia nodded, as did Cesar.

"So…" he took a deep breath, "when my wife had a stroke, I mean, that shouldn't have happened, right?" He sat for a moment, his eyes not seeing the room around him. "She had a massive stroke while I was at the clinic seeing patients. She was thirty-two. Our son was only one… not quite one. Eight months old…" He shook his head, as if shaking away the past and looked at the faces around him in the room. "Somehow she figured out how to dial 911… anyway, she had the stroke. She had massive hemorrhaging starting in the left temporal lobe. She was in a coma for weeks. Her mother came up to stay with us. With me and Brandon." Mark took a breath, and Redley nodded with encouragement.

"I couldn't do anything. I couldn't treat her. I couldn't make her well. Hell, I couldn't do anything. Anyway… after a while, they reduced the medication and she came out of the coma. She couldn't talk. She was partially paralyzed, couldn't speak. She didn't even recognize me at first."

Redley put her hand on Mark's arm.

"It was a long time ago," he said to her, reassuring her. "A long time ago."

"As you say, Mark, I know much of this," said Fletcher, "and I realize you want Julia and Redley to hear it, but I'm not sure we have the time now. I don't want to seem unfeeling, but is this relevant?"

"That was pretty rude, Fletch," said Redley. "Let him finish."

"No wait," said Mark. "He's got a point. You don't need all these details."

"Julia?" asked Cesar. "What do you think?"

"It's your agenda. It depends on how much time you all have. Stories can help us understand each other better," said Julia.

"I think I get Redley a little better after hearing the details of her story," said Cesar.

"Personal background does matter," said Julia. "Who we are as leaders and how we act and the choices we make all come from somewhere, you know."

Cesar looked at his watch. "I think we have the time. We should make the time," he said. "Okay, Fletcher?" He looked down the table and everyone nodded, including Fletcher.

Mark hesitated for a minute and then went on.

"So, the point of all this is that the town rallied round. It was amazing. There were so many casseroles in the freezer. Flowers. People visiting. People helping with my son. People doing yard work. At the clinic even. Really, amazing. I think your wife contributed quite a few," Mark said, turning to Fletcher with a small laugh. "Lasagna, I think. I had a lot of lasagna in those months."

"She did. Everyone did," said Fletcher.

"Anyway, she needed to re-learn everything. To feed herself. To talk simple words. To learn to read again. Again the town rallied round. She was in the rehab center at first. Then she came home and people came to us. Not just the PT and OT people but the townspeople. They took turns exercising her muscles at first. Then helping her at every stage. Me and Brandon, too. Meals, child care, transportation, anything we needed. We were wrapped in support, never having to ask."

He shook his head as if looking back in time. "Listen, I haven't told this story in a very long time. She was incredibly strong. She worked so hard. When she came home, she tried to be a mother, a wife. She really, really tried. The town tried to help her." He took a deep breath. Everyone waited. A truck rumbled by on the street below.

"It just wasn't going to happen. There was so much she was working on. Brandon was so active. He was learning to walk. Talking a mile a minute. Always on the go. It was too much for her."

Mark shrugged and shook his head.

"She decided she wanted a divorce. About two years after the stroke. She said she wasn't the woman I married and I deserved better. I argued and argued. Then she said she couldn't stand how impatient she was with Brandon. Didn't want him to have to live with that. She wanted to live alone. Anyway, that's what happened." Mark shrugged and looked from face to face.

"You can't just leave us with that," said Redley. "Finish the story."

"I don't want to spend more of our time on it," said Mark. "I just was telling you because of how important the people in this town were to me. Are to me. I thought they might judge us but no one did. They rallied around me, around her, around Brandon. No one took sides. I thought she'd change her mind but she never did. So, finally I gave in to her wishes and we divorced. Brandon goes to visit when he comes home."

Mark took another deep breath and let it out with a sigh. "This community was different then. We knew each other. People cared about each other. Supported each other. My family couldn't have made it without their support. That's not the case anymore. We're all so disconnected. There's no heart of the town. I want to bring it back!"

Redley reached out to put her hand on Mark's shoulder. "Geez, I'm sorry, Mark. I never knew."

He nodded briefly. "So here's the thing. We could create a real vibrant community with this building." Mark's energy seemed to shift and he sat up straighter in his chair, picking up his papers. "My pro forma shows how the building can be renovated into three distinct, but integrated areas. There would be a Youth Center. Where kids can come after school and hang out."

"If you have a youth center you should definitely have a game room. Computer games and maybe some of those tables for the imaginary games like Dungeons and Dragons," said Redley.

"My son would like that," said Fletcher, frowning.

"Great idea," said Mark. "And of course a sports center. The building is big enough for an indoor track. We need that in our climate."

"That's a great idea, Mark," said Redley. "I'd love that! I hate when the roads and sidewalks get covered in ice and I can't get out to run."

Mark nodded. "The seniors could walk it during the day. The school teams in the area could pay to use it in the afternoons for events. Basketball courts. An exercise room. We need to get people moving in this town. Counter the obesity problem. I can't stand seeing how many of the kids are overweight."

Cesar shifted in his chair. "Not just kids, Mark, I'm afraid to say. I could use a facility like that myself. I never use the treadmill at home. I joined that cheap gym in the next county, but don't go because I never find the time to get there."

"Exactly," said Mark. "We figure that we can charge a very minimal membership fee to our county residents, but charge a higher fee for outside memberships."

"How about a day fee for tourists?" asked Redley.

"Great idea," said Cesar.

"You know what else earns money," said Fletcher thoughtfully, "a hockey rink. It takes up a lot of space, but there isn't a good indoor rink around and we could rent out ice time easily. That could help pay for operating costs, don't you think?"

"That could be interesting," said Cesar. "If it will fit."

"Seems like anything and everything will fit," said Fletcher, "since that building is such an ark."

"Then for the seniors," went on Mark, "we'd have a real senior center. Activities like bridge and organized day trips. We would offer support services through there. A commercial kitchen so Meals on Wheels could operate out of it. A hot lunch program. A bereavement group. Whatever is needed. The best though, is the dining area could double as a ballroom. It would be great. Dances on Saturday nights. Lessons."

"Dances aren't just for seniors, Mark. My wife and I would love a place to ballroom dance. Could we get someone to offer lessons?" asked Cesar. Just then his phone vibrated again. He looked at the screen and then shut it off. "The high school could hold its prom there," he added thoughtfully.

"What about a computer center for the seniors?" asked Redley.

"The kids could teach the seniors," suggested Fletcher.

"Great! I love it," said Mark. "So here are the numbers."

Mark presented his pro forma with just a little help from Fletcher. When he finished, everyone applauded. He grinned. "Thanks, all. That's the last business plan presentation I make. If the town picks this idea, someone else will have to take it from here."

"Wait a minute," said Fletcher. "No one said the town was going to do the picking."

Pause and Reflect

Chapter 23

"I thought we all agreed that we were going to survey the town," said the mayor. "I specifically asked you if you agreed, Fletcher."

"You did and I did. I agreed that we should reach out to them and ask their opinion. I didn't say we should allow their opinion to rule. It's not a binding vote."

Cesar took a slow sip of the beer in front of him. He turned to Julia, shrugged, then turned back to Fletcher. "Okay. I should get curious here, right? Tell me what you mean."

"We're the accountable ones. Yes, ask their opinion. Let them know some of the choices we're considering to get them involved. Their awareness and involvement is important, I agree. It's still our responsibility, though, to make the final decision," said Fletcher. "Just like at the bank. As the CEO, I have final accountability."

"So, even if the townspeople are all in favor of one plan, you think we could ignore that and choose another?" asked Mark.

Fletcher nodded. "If we didn't think it was right, yes. Definitely. It's the role of leaders to make the best decisions they can with the information they have, even if that decision isn't popular."

Cesar shifted to Julia, who was sitting at the other end of the table. She had a cup of beer in front of her, but hadn't touched it. "What do you say to this, Julia? I see Fletcher's point, but how can we go out to the town and then ignore their decision?"

"You really don't need me to think this through. You both make good points."

"But what do you think?" asked Mark. "What's your view of the leader's role in this case?"

Julia looked around the table. "Like I said, both Fletcher and Cesar have made good points. Leaders have to make unpopular decisions at times," said Julia. "That's why leadership can be so lonely. You all know that. You hold the highest level of accountability."

Everyone nodded.

"On the other hand, you need the support of the people in the town for whatever you do. If you ask people's opinions and you totally ignore them, why should they trust you? After all, it's their town, too. If they don't want a community center and you put one there, will it succeed?"

"That's right," said Mark. "If we're not going to pay attention to their opinion, I wonder whether we should even ask for it. We could just have information meetings. Part of the reason for engaging them was to build support for our process, remember?"

"We'd have to be damn careful about how we frame it up, telling them why we were asking them. That's for sure," said Redley. "Pass me the sausage and green pepper, Mark, will you?"

Mark flipped open a pizza box and passed it to Redley. "It's the last one," he said. "Finish it."

Redley took the piece and put it on her plate. "Look, maybe Mark's right. Maybe we should just keep going along without them, ignore the crap in the paper about us, ignore the town opinion. You know, just do it ourselves."

"I'm not saying we shouldn't ask or that we are going to totally ignore their opinion," said Fletcher, slight annoyance creeping into his voice. "What I'm saying is that we still have the fiduciary responsibility to make the final decision. We will always have more information accessible to us than them. We can't present everything to them. We may need to tell them what's best for them. Right, Julia?"

Julia leaned forward. They all turned and waited. Cesar nodded.

"Maybe," she said. "It's another choice you'll all have to make together. I'll just point out the way you each come at it from a different perspective based on who you are and your experience of the world. Look at you, Redley, with the background you just shared with us, experimenting in your basement. Selling at concerts. Building your business without bank support. It makes sense you'd be willing to just do it without outside input. And, Mark has talked about the importance of the community to him in his life. No wonder he would want to include the community. I can't say about Fletcher because I haven't heard his story."

"I don't see where you're going this time, Julia," said Cesar.

"I'm just encouraging you all to notice the way your experiences could influence your leadership values and choices. Your background influences your perspective. It's a filter you look through."

"What do we do about it, though?" asked Cesar.

"Use the knowledge to understand yourself and one another better. Rather than operating from a default, it might give you more choices."

"That makes sense to me," said Redley. "Mark? Chief?"

They both nodded.

"In a way, it's that same idea about change occurring when you focus more on where you are now," finished Julia. "Remember the paradox of it? Paying careful attention to who and how you are right now can move you out of automatic pilot and give you more choices."

"Yeah," said Redley, wrapping her hair up into a bun and sticking a pencil into it to hold it in place. "There's a downside to choice, right? You know that story about the centipede?"

Mark shook his head, Fletcher frowned.

Cesar laughed. "Okay, I'll bite. Is this a joke?"

"No. The centipede was walking along easily when a worm came up to him and asked him how he knew which foot to start out with. 'I don't know,' he said, 'let me think about it.' From then on, he couldn't move because he was plagued with the choice."

"Okay," said the mayor. "I say we leave our choice of how to handle the town's feedback until later so we can move on now. Let's come back to this again after we hear Fletcher's presentation." The mayor looked from one face to another. "Do we all agree?" Everyone nodded. "Are you ready to present, Fletcher?"

Pause and Reflect

Chapter 24

Fletcher put down the piece of crust he was finishing and dusted off his hands, then wiped them on a napkin. He slid folders from his briefcase that sat on the floor next to him and passed them around the table, then loosened his tie.

"Wow," said Redley, noticing. "You're finally getting casual." She grinned and elbowed him. He rolled his eyes and picked up his own papers, but he laughed.

"This is my pro forma for the performing arts center. I've got a budget for rehab that includes a world-class acoustic hall. It's modeled after one in Australia that's designed to be flexible in size, allowing intimate small concerts and very large symphony or jazz and rock...," he turned to Redley, "performances. It is designed to take advantage of the view of the river that the building has. So, unlike many concert halls, it has a wall of glass. Surrounding the hall are smaller rooms for music lessons and practice rooms."

"What about some tie-in with the schools and the colleges?" asked Cesar.

"Right, Mayor," said Fletcher. "I've had some conversations with the school superintendent and they are very interested. The university has its own performing arts building but the acoustics aren't as good as this will be. What's available now in computer modeling of sound transmission allows for a far superior result. So, they would be interested in renting the space for certain types of concerts." Fletcher started coughing and reached for the bottle in front of him but it was empty.

Redley took another beer out of the cooler at her feet and offered it to Fletcher. He nodded and she flipped the top off and handed it to him.

"I'll have another," said Mark.

"Me, too," said Cesar.

Redley handed out two more beers and looked over at Julia.

"Not me, thanks. I'm not much of a beer drinker, although the sip I had of this one was delicious."

Redley laughed. "How about trying some mead? I brought a bottle." Before Julia could answer, she had the bottle open and was pouring some into a small plastic cup. Julia accepted it and took a small sip. "This is lavender mead," said Redley.

"Interesting. I've never had mead. Quite a treat." She took another sip, obviously enjoying it more than the beer.

"Come visit the brewery and I'll give you a tour of how it's made. Sorry, Fletch," said Redley. "Didn't mean to interrupt your flow. Go on."

"So, here's where it gets interesting. I've been able to find some data that supports my assumption that a cultural center would be an attraction for the growth of a wealthy demographic. Sarasota, Florida shows up often as an example."

"Sarasota has a variety of the arts represented," said Mark. "My parents used to have a condo down there. But, I worry about the viability of an orchestra. Isn't classical music sort of, I don't know… dying out?"

"No," said Fletcher. "As a matter of fact, I've found out that 12% of all iTunes downloads are classical music. So, it's clearly not a dying interest. As for attracting wealth and economic growth, in Boston they have attributed $166 million of economic activity to the Boston Symphony."

"We can't compare ourselves to the Boston Symphony, Fletch," said Redley. "They've been around since the late eighteen hundreds."

"Certainly not," responded Fletcher. "But wait. How did you know that?"

Redley just shrugged.

"Anyway, it's attracting charitable funds as well. In 2010, arts giving increased by 5.7% for a total of $13.3 billion." He paused for effect. "More important, think of the impact this orchestra and a cultural center would have on the schools. I found research that says that when students are immersed in an arts program, their academic performance and results on standardized testing increased twelve percent."

"That sounds important to our community," commented Mark. "Is there a way to attract more younger people to concerts? It seems like symphonies always attract a more mature audience."

"Yes, there is," said Fletcher, sitting up in his seat. "Actually the demographic of eighteen to thirty-four is the third largest in classical music audiences." Fletcher explained that his research had discovered that ticketing policies turn younger people away, because the don't want to be committed to a ticket subscription. They prefer flexibility and last minute possibilities.

"So we make sure to have a variety of flexible subscriptions and ticket offerings. Student discounts, of course. Educating the audience so they can enjoy the music more knowledgeably. Also the way it's branded. Marketing and image."

"Just like with any business," said Redley.

"Exactly," said Fletcher with a nod. "There are tie-in possibilities. I've done some research and discovered that downtowns with housing become more alive. I think we should consider some luxury rental units in one end of the building opposite from the concert hall and practice rooms. It would be ongoing income to support the maintenance of the whole building. On the ground floor we could have uses that wouldn't disturb the residents. We'd have small gallery and working art studio spaces that could be leased to local artists and crafts people. You asked about the university, Mayor. What the university has wanted but doesn't have is a radio station. I've included a broadcast studio in the plans. They'd rent it from us for additional ongoing income."

"What a great idea," said the mayor.

"Cool," said Redley. "I wonder. Could it also be used for recording? I see a lot of garage bands making their own CD's now. That could be another source of income."

Fletcher nodded. "I don't know but we could find out. Seems like a good idea. I'd like the symphony to make recordings anyway. Sell them after concerts. Another source of income."

"Good marketing, too," added Redley. "Increases visibility."

"Increasing ticket sales, right?" said Fletcher.

"Exactly."

"What about the rehearsals?" asked Mark. "When I was a kid growing up in New York, my school used to take us on field trips into Manhattan to see rehearsals of the New York Met and the Philharmonic."

"Great idea," said Fletcher.

"I have an idea," said Julia suddenly.

They all turned to her, expecting a comment on their process. "I thought we were doing well," said Fletcher.

"You were, and I'm glad you noticed," said Julia with a smile. "My idea has to do with your performing arts center."

"Oh," said Fletcher, sounding surprised. "Oh."

"I sometimes vacation on Cape Cod, and in two different venues, one a theatre and one a movie house, they broadcast live opera performances from the Met in New York. It's quite popular."

"You don't usually join in with the content, Julia," said Redley in a teasing tone. "I thought you were all about our process."

"Look at that," said Julia. "You see it's hard to stay out of a conversation when the content gets really interesting to you."

"I'm glad you're interested," said Fletcher.

Julia nodded and smiled, but turned back to Redley. "Thank you for catching that."

"Come on," said Cesar. "Why can't you join into the content, too?"

"It's not that I can't, it's just not my job. The content is your responsibility and my role is to increase your awareness of your process. If I get too interested or too emotionally engaged with the content, I lose my focus on process."

All four of them sat with confused looks.

"Think about it. You're very skilled in the content of your work. But, as leaders, I'm trying to increase your ability to also engage with your process. To see what's happening in the *way* you interact with each other. If it's going well, fine."

They all nodded. "So if it's not going well," prompted Redley.

"If not, you've been learning techniques to get back on track, right? So as leaders, you want to be skilled enough to shift back and forth constantly between the content and the process. Like the orchestra conductor paying attention to the score and the notes, but also the pacing, the entrances and exits and crescendos, the passion of the musicians."

They all nodded.

"But, my only job is to check your process. So anyway, I'm interrupting here. See how my comment got us off track?"

"But it was a good idea," said Fletcher. "I didn't know that live opera video feed was happening. That would be great. I couldn't figure out how to include opera. And I can't think why it didn't occur to me before this, but of course we could have theater and films as well. We haven't had an art film house in this area for years. Just the mega-plex at the mall in the next county."

Fletcher reviewed the rest of his numbers on symphony salaries, insurance, etc., and data on demographics of symphony supporters, then concluded. "This is a sure win for this town."

They all sat looking at him, as if waiting for something more.

Pause and Reflect

Chapter 25

"What?" Fletcher asked finally. "What have I forgotten?"

"I had a pretty personal reason for my plan," observed Mark. "Redley has a personal attachment to her plan. Julia says that understanding how our experience influences our choices is a good thing. I'm curious about where your interest in music comes from."

"Logic and common sense," said Fletcher.

"Right," said Redley, a little sarcastically.

"What does that mean?" asked Fletcher abruptly.

She sighed. "When it comes right down to it, does logic and common sense really rule? All the research says that we make decisions based on emotion and then rationalize them with logic and common sense. So, what's the emotion involved here, Fletch?"

"I think you ought to leave it alone, Redley," said Cesar. "Look at Fletcher. You're obviously making him uncomfortable."

"She's not making me anything," said Fletcher crossly.

"Let's move on," said Cesar, just as his phone vibrated again. He picked it up.

"If Fletcher has completely finished," said Mark, filling in the awkward gap, "maybe we should return to the discussion about how we bring all this to the community."

"How about if we take a five minute break," said the mayor. "My wife has called three times. I need to see if there's an emergency or something with the family." He started out into the hall. "Why don't you all decide whether you want to keep going or finish up for this evening and leave the community survey planning for the next meeting."

After he left, Redley turned to Julia. "This meeting seemed so good. We all advocated for our plans just like in the past. I don't get why this felt so different."

Fletcher and Mark nodded.

"I like your curiosity. I can tell you what I saw, but maybe we could wait for the mayor?" asked Julia.

"We need to decide about the rest of this meeting agenda," said Mark.

"As far as I'm concerned, we've done enough tonight," said Fletcher. "I'd like to go home when the mayor gets back. Take up the survey when we meet early next week."

"That's what I was thinking," said Mark. "How about you?" he asked Redley.

"Totally. I'm beat."

"Sorry for the interruption, folks," said Cesar, as he walked back in. "I couldn't get through to my wife after all. She didn't leave a message so it can't be too urgent. Now, where were we?"

"We're done with the business part of the meeting, if it's okay with you, Chief," said Redley. "But we were asking Julia why this meeting felt so much better."

Cesar nodded and looked to Julia.

"I'm not sure anything was different," said Fletcher. "We just had more information to share. What do you say, Julia?"

"Well," she responded. "You were all more detailed, that's true. But that's not only what made this a more effective meeting. There were several things. First of all, you had a clear goal you had all agreed upon in advance and prepared for. The mayor framed it up. You knew what you were expected to do in this one meeting. No decision was being asked for, just a full and complete discussion on each plan, right?"

"Yes," said Fletcher. "Just as I said. We had more information."

"It was more than that, Fletcher. You knew you weren't going to have to make a decision. No choice was involved. It was about sharing and brainstorming. You were all clear on the intent. It was not about convincing each other."

"A-ha," said Redley. "I get it. In fact, I could feel it. I felt different as I talked about my plan. I didn't feel like I had to convince or defend. Same when I listened to the other plans."

Mark nodded. "I agree. Okay, so we had a clear and shared purpose. What else? Or was it just that?"

Julia took a sip of her mead. "Remember I talked about how birds in a flock scatter if a hawk enters their midst? The danger makes them forget each other at first. But, they never go too far or for too long. Then, they re-gather. How do they do that? I've actually looked into the rules of how they fly together, because it seems so easy and graceful but if you watch them they shift their positions relative to one another all the time. When they re-gather after scattering, they never crash into each other like people do. It's hard to see why it works. So I found that some computer guy did a model and discovered three rules they follow. Fletcher, you mentioned how they use computers now for acoustic modeling?" Fletcher nodded. She took a breath and looked around the table. Everyone looked back, seeming interested, but slightly confused.

"This will make sense in a minute, I promise," she assured them. "So this researcher tried to find the fewest number of rules that would allow computer generated birds to flock like real ones. He came up with three, all around how they pay attention to where they are relative to each other. The three rules they follow are fly toward their average setting, fly to avoid crowding one another, and fly toward the average position of local flock-mates."

"I don't get it. What's the relevance?" asked Fletcher.

"I thought if I could figure out three rules for people working together like this guy did for the birds, I'd be able to help teams be more successful together. Those are the three rules I had the mayor write on the flip chart during that first meeting I attended. What I noticed tonight is you all seemed to follow those three rules."

"I'm embarrassed to say I've forgotten them," said Mark. "We kept our distance so we weren't up and moving around the room bumping into each other?"

Julia laughed. "Sort of. Look, the first one is the first thing we talked about when we first started working together.

Ask questions, real questions, and notice whether you are getting answers. You all did that in spades tonight. It happens naturally when you get interested, but there are times working in groups when you have to notice and work to make that happen. It keeps you in relation to one another."

"We did do that, I noticed that a lot," said Mark. "What else?"

"Taking your share of time and your share of responsibility for success," said Julia. "All too often in groups everyone leaves the responsibility to someone else. Often it's the leader, and sometimes it's the most vocal member of the team."

"That is so true," said Redley. "I hate when one person takes it on him or herself to dominate the conversation."

"That tends to be what we notice," said Julia. "But it's just as unfair for someone to stay quiet. We all have something to contribute. You all took part this evening. Everyone, in each part of the discussion. And all the comments weren't going through your leader, the mayor. You talked easily to one another."

She paused and they all nodded, remembering. "The last thing is hard for me to notice from the outside, but I think you were all doing it. Just the fact that you felt the meeting was different tonight gave me a clue, Redley."

"What?" asked Redley. "What do you mean? Wasn't the third rule something about cameras?"

Julia laughed. "Shifting your focus. Taking time to stay aware of what's going on in the group, and what's going on inside you. From big picture to details and back."

"We did that?" asked Mark.

"You went from talking about your overall concepts and the impact on the town to little details of design and back again to impact. You all kept look around at each other's faces, at their body language. You seemed to react to changes of energy and pace."

"That's like what you told me to do with my assistant," said Fletcher.

"Exactly, but this time it's with the whole group. A group or a team has an energy all of its own, and you also have the individual reaction of each of you."

"Didn't you also say something about turning the focus on yourself?" asked Redley.

"Paying attention to that feeling you had that something was different tonight is an example," answered Julia. "Any of you play poker?"

Only Fletcher nodded.

"Well, there was a study on people playing poker. When the dealer stacked the deck, people would start getting a sensation in their palms long before their rational mind noticed. Once they were told to pay attention to the physical sensations, they did much better in noticing and then adjusting their strategy."

"That's amazing!" said Redley. Fletcher look very interested.

"Make sense to me. The body is highly reactive," said Mark.

Julia nodded. "A great source of information. Thoughts, feelings, tense muscles in your shoulders or stomach, instinct, whatever. It can provide great clues to act upon. For example, if you sense frustration, or curiosity, you can take action that may help the group. Or action that can help you. Either way, it's an informed intentional choice. Not just a blow up that catches you unaware."

"I can identify with that," said Mark ruefully.

"So say the three rules again," said Cesar, "and then we should wrap up."

"Okay," said Julia. "I'll give you the shorthand version. Ask questions, share time, and keep adjusting your focus. How's that?"

"Great," said Cesar.

"Okay, Chief," said Redley, "I'll get busy on the survey with my folks."

"Wait, was that decision made about survey results?" asked the mayor.

"I think we should at least get it ready," said Redley.

"In the meantime we can all think about how to use the results," added Mark.

Cesar looked from face to face. Everyone was nodding their agreement. "Fine," he said. "We can review it when we meet next, plus go over any other action we want to take." He looked around the table, making eye contact with each person. "You've all done some great work, both preparing for tonight and adding to one another's ideas. You should be proud of yourselves."

"You too, Mayor," said Mark.

They started picking up the mess on the table. "Who wants leftovers?" asked Redley.

"Not me," said Mark and Cesar in unison.

"Fletcher?" asked Redley.

He looked at the boxes. "I guess so. My son's with me tonight. In fact, I have to pick him up from band practice shortly. He's always hungry."

They finished cleaning up. Mark hurried out to take his dog for a walk. Redley said she was going back to the brewery to finish up some work and reminded Julia to come by for a tour.

"Tomorrow morning too soon?" Julia asked. "Or do you have too much to catch up on?"

"I always have too much to do, so it won't matter which day. I don't have meetings tomorrow until eleven, so come early and we'll have coffee together," invited Redley as she left.

Fletcher asked Julia where she'd parked.

"In the lot down the street," she said.

"I'll walk with you," he offered. "I'm parked there, too, and I have something brief I'd like to talk with you about."

Chapter 26

F letcher balanced the pizza box and his papers and tried to hold the door for Julia. She chuckled and took the pizza box from him.

"Let me help," she said. They walked through the door and into the still night air.

"I owe you an apology, Julia," said Fletcher.

"Oh?"

"I'm always very skeptical of consultants. You're the first one that I..." he paused, "that I..." He was silent and their footsteps on the pavement echoed against the buildings.

"That you what?" asked Julia, finally.

"You've made a difference in this team. I'm still not quite sure how, but I can see it. Helped me see the situation with Angie a little better."

"Is it better?"

"She took back her letter of resignation, at least. Fair's fair. I wanted to tell you."

"Thank you, Fletcher. I appreciate hearing it." They had gotten to the parking lot and Julia handed Fletcher back the pizza box.

Fletcher took the box and looked at it for a moment.

"This pizza's for my son. Not sure if he'll appreciate it, coming from me. I'm sure if he could quit being my son right now, he would."

"How old is he?" Julia asked.

"Fifteen," said Fletcher. "Know anything about teenagers, Julia?"

She laughed and shook her head. "Life with my own teens was confusing. Thankfully, as with all teens, eventually they grew up. I liked working with teens though. You never knew what would come next. They didn't know either. It made me pay more attention to what was happening in the moment because I couldn't ever anticipate. Maybe that's partly why I enjoyed working with them."

Fletcher shook his head. "I'm not sure I'd go along with your preference right now."

"You know I read once that if you give one of those psychological Rorschach tests to a teen, they come out with the same profile as a schizophrenic?"

"I can believe that," grumbled Fletcher. "He's just so negative. We fight about everything. I don't know why my ex-wife can't set down more rules and why it always has to be me."

"You fight about everything?" repeated Julia.

"You know. The usual stuff. Homework. How he dresses. How much time he plays video games."

"But you said you're picking him up from band practice. That can't be bad."

"That's because I require him to play an instrument."

"You do?" she asked. "Huh…." Julia was quiet for a minute and Fletcher was lost in his own thoughts. She looked up at him. "Would you mind if I asked why?"

"Why what?"

"Why you require him to play an instrument?"

"Look, you heard the statistics on kids' academics improving if they're involved with the arts."

"I did. Does it work for him?"

"I don't know. But he's going to play."

"Sounds very important to you," said Julia softly. She fished her keys out of her purse and unlocked the door to her car.

"It is. I always wanted to play an instrument. My older sister had a flute and I loved to try playing it."

"Ahh," said Julia. "Did you ever get to play it?"

"My father wouldn't let me. Too feminine. A waste of time. Go to business school, he said. Join the bank, he said. So I did. But I started taking lessons three years ago. I thought it would be a good motivator for my son."

"Was it?"

"No," said Fletcher simply. "But I still enjoy it. "

"Why?" asked Julia. "What do you enjoy about it?"

Fletcher stopped and closed his eyes for a minute, swaying just slightly. Then, he opened his eyes and smiled. "It's difficult to put into words. Total focus is required. Sometimes it's extremely hard and often very frustrating. Even so, it always takes me... I don't know... out of myself."

"You know, Fletcher," said Julia. "I'm wondering why you didn't tell any of this to the committee. I think they would have..."

"No. It's private."

"Have you told your son all that? Why you play?"

"No. Why I play? That would sound silly to him. Besides it's irrelevant."

Julia shrugged. "If you want people to understand you, if you want to influence them, the why is very important, that's all." Julia opened her car door and slid into the front seat. "I take it your son doesn't much like it."

"No he doesn't. It's not like I forced him to play the flute. I gave him a choice of any instrument. First it was the tuba. Then sax. Now it's trumpet. Fine, as long as he plays. All we do is fight about it."

"Is it worth it?" she said, looking up at him.

"What do you mean?"

"Does it help your relationship? Does it make him a better person? Does it make him a better musician?"

Fletcher was silent. "I guess I'd have to say no, no, and no."

"Are you interested in some advice?"

"Yes. I guess that's what I was hoping for," admitted Fletcher ruefully.

"Do you remember after I had that interaction with the mayor when he was so upset with me early on in one of our meetings?"

Fletcher nodded. "I did. You didn't argue."

"Exactly. I didn't. I didn't want to make him more resistant to me. I just got curious. I asked questions."

"I've asked my son lots of questions but he just keeps arguing. It doesn't change anything." Fletcher's voice was getting harsher.

"Okay, think of it another way. Remember when I was talking about the strange paradox around where change needs to start?" she asked.

"Yes… I think…. Was it the thing about why AA works for people? They have to accept where they are before they can help themselves."

"Pretty much. Rather than trying to force change, you start with accepting what is. In this case, you say your son doesn't want to play. Maybe he doesn't want to be forced to play. He wants to play video games. Could you accept that for now?"

"No! There's no future in video games!" said Fletcher emphatically.

"Actually, there is indeed. But that's not the point. Not at all. I'm just wondering if you could appreciate his skill in that for now. Similar to how you're working at appreciating your assistant."

"Oh, Julia. You're asking a lot."

"I'm not asking anything. I'm just wondering whether you are interested in trying something different, if what you're doing isn't working?"

"I'll think about it," said Fletcher, looking down at the pizza box he held. "I will."

He said goodbye to Julia, and got into his own car. He was startled by the voice that came on the radio when he turned the ignition key.

Chapter 27

The mayor walked out of the back door of the town hall where his car was parked in his private space. He started the car and the radio came on. He heard a familiar voice. The local reporter was talking about the mill building and the grant process. Cesar turned up the volume, sitting listening without even putting his car in gear.

"This may not be a building worth saving," said the reporter, "but the site has great value and should be used in a way that will bring the most economic benefit to the town. A local news blog reports they have sources that say a collaboration is being formed between one of our state's largest commercial developers and a highly successful Las Vegas casino operator. The blogger goes on to report the grant money the mayor is chasing is unlikely to be a reasonable possibility and new collaborators may be able to come up with a proposal for our town that will be a far more lucrative short term and long term win, bringing hundreds of good paying jobs into town and our surroundings. Tune in for more as soon as we get it."

Cesar gripped the steering wheel tightly. "We've got to stop this," he hissed. "Now that damn blogger has the regular reporters going."

He put the car in gear and chewed on the news report all the whole way home, until he turned into the driveway and started to worry about why his wife had called.

She was just fine, sitting in their den at her computer. She looked up at him with a worried smile.

"What's going on, Kelly?" he said. "You called three times. I tried to call you back but you didn't answer."

"Mel Schroom called for you. He was very insistent he needed to talk to you."

"Who???"

"You know. Mel Schroom. That reporter, or blogger or whatever he is that drives you crazy. Several times he called. You'll probably have messages at your office because he said he was calling there, too. I wasn't going to give him your cell phone number."

"How did he get the house phone? I don't like that. We're unlisted." The mayor walked over to the desk and kissed the top of her head absentmindedly.

"Oh no, that's not enough," she said and turned and pulled him down to her for a full kiss. When she let go he half-smiled and held her chin a minute with his hand. Then he straightened up.

"What did Mr. Schroom want?"

"I don't know," she said. "He just said it was urgent. He wanted to get your comment on some information he had. I must have been putting the cat out for the night when you called me. I've been here all evening."

"Damn. What could possibly be urgent?"

"I don't know. He didn't say it was urgent the first two times. Maybe he just didn't like the fact that you never get back to him."

"I never what??? Not you, Kelly. Are you suddenly on his side?"

"No! It's not about sides. I was offering you a possibility that your own behavior might be contributing to Schroom's attitude."

"This isn't about me. Why are you making it about me?"

"Come on, Cesar! You're doing it again."

"Doing what?" he asked, leaning against the doorway with exaggerated patience.

"Never mind," Kelly said quickly.

"Oh, no, you're not going to get away with that. Tell me."

"It's just that when you're unhappy you always blame what the other person is doing."

"So now this is about you? About us?" said Cesar slowly.

Kelly sighed and stood up, and walked over to Cesar, standing just inches away.

"I'm not the enemy here, Cesar," she whispered gently.

He took her in his arms with a big growl. "I know, Kel," he said into her ear. "Go on and say what you wanted to say. I'm listening."

She nestled into his shoulder, her words slightly muffled. "I just wanted to point out that there's two sides to every story, right? Whether it's you and me, or you and Schroom. Don't you think?"

"I know, I know. You're right as always. Come on, let's go to bed."

"Okay, just let me finish my email and I'll shut the computer down," said Kelly, kissing him quickly and sliding out of his arms to go back to her desk.

"Oooooh," said Kelly as she tapped a few keys on her computer. "I have his blog pulled up and there's a new post. You're not going to like it. Look." She turned the computer screen so he could see.

"I don't have my glasses. Read it to me."

"Okay, but don't shoot the messenger. Hmmm. Let's see. 'Due to the mayor's poorly named Blue Ribbon Committee's dragging their heels, this large building in our town continues as an eyesore. The composition of the committee makes us all wonder about the size of their donations, as not one of the three of them has any development experience. In spite of frequent calls to the mayor he has made himself unavailable for questions. We wonder what he's trying to hide. Now we have reports that he's brought in a consultant at top dollar. Throwing good money after bad. This site has great value and should be used in a way that will bring the most economic benefit to the town. They should be considering the possibilities that a casino could create, with new jobs and economic development. Should the mayor disband the Blue Ribbon Committee and let someone else's money, a skilled private developer, create a new tax paying business with lots of good job opportunities? Send your comments.' That's all."

Cesar was pacing back and forth as she read. "That's all? That's all? That's preposterous. Mel Schroom. What a name.

Sounds like mushroom. Toadstool. That's what he is. He's a toadstool."

"Now, Honey…"

"He's slandering my committee! Making us look incompetent. Making me look irrational or unethical. Did he really imply they bought their position? What kind of crap is that? Who the hell would donate money so they could give up their time to be on this committee that pays nothing? He's just out for himself."

"How does he benefit from this? Why would you say that?" asked Kelly.

"How do I know? Maybe there really is a casino developer in the wings and he's paying Mr. Toadstool to stir up dirt. Just like he stirred up dirt during my campaign."

"That was pretty unpleasant, I know."

"Unpleasant??" The word burst from Cesar's mouth with a fine shower of saliva. "It was worse than unpleasant! He almost cost me the election. How can you defend him?"

"I'm not defending him! Are you really yelling at me, Cesar?" Kelly half stood up.

Cesar ran his hands through his dark hair. "Sorry. Sorry. Look what he's doing to me. He makes me crazy." He went over and pulled his wife from her chair and took her in his arms. He rested his chin on her head and sighed. "What am I going to do? It cost us a small fortune to clean up his mess last time."

"This is different, Honey." Kelly pulled away only enough to look up at her husband. "This isn't about your past. This is about the present. You don't have to hire a lawyer or produce evidence. You need a strategy. Maybe Julia could help."

"Oh great. Then he'll accuse me of spending even more money."

Kelly stayed silent, her eye contact with him steady.

Finally he pulled her back against him. "Fine. I know when to stop fighting. I'll call Julia in the morning."

Chapter 28

The next morning Julia made her way across town to the brewery. Redley ushered her into her office and poured coffee for them both. They took their cups to the window overlooking the water and Redley pointed out some landmarks.

"I think you'll get wet when you leave, Julia," said Redley. "I hope you parked close."

"Winter's been winding down with too many weeks of this cold damp gray, hasn't it," Julia answered, as they looked at the dark clouds on the horizon.

"I'm glad you came to work with the committee," said Redley.

"I'm enjoying myself," said Julia. "But that's really not a response to your comment. Thank you."

"You're making a difference. We were stuck before you."

"It's always good to have feedback. Especially good feedback. I'm glad you think it's helping."

"Plus it's nice to have another woman in the room," said Redley.

Julia nodded thoughtfully. "It must be hard, being a woman in such a male dominated field. Until you talked about it last night, I never thought about it."

"You know, it isn't so hard now. It was at first. I had a few employees that didn't respect a woman. But that's a while ago now."

"What's changed?" asked Julia.

"I guess two things happened. I toughened up, and it also got easier as the business grew and I got more confident. Now people are a whole lot more interested in the beer and the mead than they are in me."

"I'm interested in hearing more about both the beer and mead," said Julia, finishing her coffee.

They walked out of the office and Redley was stopped by one of her employees with a marketing question.

"The new tap handle designs are in, Boss Lady. When do you want to review them?"

Redley made an appointment for later that morning.

"Our tap handles were being commandeered by some of these little craft breweries. Everyone thinks they can make beer these days," said Redley with disgust. "They can't afford to do it properly so they cut corners. They were getting our handles from the distributors and just covering our name with a label. We have to redesign the shape of the handle and where our name goes to make it harder for other companies to repurpose them."

"I see those handles and never give them a thought. I didn't know they came from the brewers," said Julia.

Further down the hall Redley was stopped by someone in a cubicle asking a payroll question and she took a moment to answer it. Someone else asked a question about a new shipping requirement in a neighboring state.

"It's so complicated to ship wine and beer across state lines," Redley told Julia. "Each state is different. We're so heavily taxed and regulated. I needed a federal winery permit for the mead and a brewer's permit for the beer. When I only made mead, I couldn't keep any grain on the premises. Nothing for beer. I did make hopped mead, though. That was fun. Still do."

"They let you have hops? Aren't they for beer?" asked Julia.

"Hops are a flower, not a grain," explained Redley. "We want to get it locally, but the local farmers can't supply us year round yet."

Another employee interrupted their progress with a question about an upcoming event. "It's the Boston Beer Fest," Redley explained to Julia. "We have two booths there, one for the beer and one for the mead."

The questions continued as they slowly made progress, Redley introducing Julia each time. By the time they got to the door of the brewery floor, she'd been stopped seven times.

"It's impressive how you're involved and on top of every detail of the business, Redley," said Julia.

"Thanks, but I struggle to keep up."

They walked through a huge warehouse full of shining stainless steel vats and under large flexible pipes carrying the beer in varying stages of completion. The concrete floor was wet. "Both from condensation and from cleaning," Redley explained.

She pointed out a big metal boxed pipe at the wall. "That's for the malted barley. Like a grain elevator. We get it delivered in huge quantities, imported from England, and that's filled outside."

They walked around a number of large wooden tubs. "These are called mash tuns," she said. "The malt comes into those and we spin it with water, all local untreated water, and extract the wort. That's the liquid that we steep over there in the brew kettles." She pointed to big tall brick columns topped with green copper and led Julia past. The heat emanated from them.

"Is there a by-product?" asked Julia.

"We've had a local farmer take it for years. Same guy."

"What does he use it for? Fertilizer?"

"No, cattle feed. Here, let's go next door." They walked through an opening into another huge warehouse space full of vats. "These are the fermentation tanks. These are kept cold with glycol circulating through them."

Several brewers were about, dressed in shorts and T-shirts and high rubber boots.

One stopped Redley. "I've got three choices for you to taste," he said.

"I'll be back in a bit," answered Redley. She directed Julia up a metal stairway and across a catwalk where she pointed down at the first vat topped with puffy pale beige foam. "That one has just had the yeast added."

"Where do you get the yeast?" asked Julia. "Is it like bread yeast?"

"Sort of. We actually keep using the same yeast. We skim it off, refrigerate it and use it again."

"Like those sourdough bread starters?" asked Julia.

"Exactly." Redley continued along the catwalk and pointed down into the vats where the top foam got progressively darker and less and less puffy. The final vat was quite dark. "That one's ready," said Redley. "They'll empty it and then get in and clean it."

"You mean they clean these by hand?" asked Julia, looking across the many vats.

"Yup," said Redley. "They get in wearing their rubber boots and scrub away. It takes about an hour to clean a tank. Then we start all over again."

"Lot of work," said Julia.

"It's like any typical small manufacturing business, Julia. Our overhead is pretty high as a percent of sales. Particularly in the brewery where we have brewers on hand pretty constantly. It's a little easier in the mead room."

They went through the tasting room. Julia looked around at all the articles of clothing and home items for sale. There were hats and shirts and jackets and candles, and neon signs, and do-it-yourself beer making kits.

"This is quite a store you have here," said Julia.

"We do okay with the tour bus business in season. Plus we have an online store. We sell much more online than we do with traffic in the store. I'd like it to be busier right here."

She led the way through an open corridor where Redley was stopped with a question about T-shirt logos. "I'm sorry, Julia," apologized Redley. "I'd say I wished we'd picked a slower time but there never is a slower time. I'm always bombarded with interruptions. It's overwhelming. But I guess it's part of my job. Let's go next door and I'll show you the mead."

Julia nodded and they walked on, with Redley explaining the process and all the uses for each piece of equipment and introducing her staff as they came up with questions. Julia noticed that the floor in the mead room was sticky.

"We use a lot of honey, all locally grown," said Redley. "We get it in five gallon pails, raw, still with pollen in it. In this first room in those tall things that look a bit like stainless rockets, we take the honey and water and ferment it with yeast. We keep those going constantly, which keeps the yeast always working. We feed the sugar water in the bottom, and take the fermented honey water out the top in those tubes."

Julia looked over the room. "Is this the same yeast as the beer?"

Redley shook her head. "No, this is a strain we got from a South African root. We've used it the last four years because it's capable of consuming all the sugar. Most meads people find are too sweet. We make drier varieties. That's why I think we've been successful at it."

"I didn't know mead was popular," said Julia.

"It's not, really. At least not in the US. Not yet. Some say it's the world's oldest fermented beverage. It's very popular still in Eastern Europe, particularly Poland, and also in South Africa. You know it's where the term honeymoon came from?"

Redley explained the early tradition that when a couple married they were given enough mead to last a month, intended to encourage the creation of their first child. "Thus, honey moon," explained Redley, with a grin.

"Sounds like fun!" said Julia, grinning back.

The next room they entered was larger, with big plastic vats encased in metal cages. "These are the fermenting tanks. This is where we flavor some of the meads. We pump the honey water onto strawberries that have been frozen to break down their cellular walls, or those over there are lavender we get locally. I like to think we help the local farmers stay in business."

A young man came in and asked Redley a question about the tasting glasses. "We're almost out, Boss, because that Mexican restaurant that ordered the custom mead bought four cases. You had said something about etching them with a new logo design. Should I re-order or wait?"

"I'll stop back after I finish with our guest." said Redley, and then introduced Julia and explained about custom mead. "The owners of the Mexican restaurant chain in the southern part of the state wanted a special tamarind mead. They supplied the tamarind, we made the mead. That's the kind of thing I'd love to see if we had more restaurants in town. Wouldn't it be great?"

Redley brought Julia through the bottling and labeling area where she was interrupted with another question.

When they'd finished the tour with the shipping room and returned to Redley's office, they sat down again in the two mismatched wing chairs in front of the desk.

"More coffee?" asked Redley.

Julia shook her head. "That was fascinating," said Julia. "I've never been through a brewery or a meadery before. Thank you for the tour."

"You're most welcome. I love giving tours. Mostly the staff does it now. We do them in both warehouses on Saturdays. When I do it, I get to see it through someone else's eyes and it reminds me how far we've come. You know, I just feel so proud of this place."

"You should," agreed Julia.

"Of my team, too. It's like my child. They're my family. Probably part of the reason I haven't found the time to have kids of my own yet. It's so time consuming. I wish I could keep it in check, sometimes. I'm never off."

"Being an entrepreneur is a non-stop job, isn't it?" agreed Julia.

"All these questions and interruptions during the day make it impossible to get anything done so I end up staying late at night to finish paperwork and new proposals and that sort of thing. Then, I feel like I'm neglecting my husband, which he complains about, so I know it's true. We thought about having him join the business but... I don't know. Didn't seem like a good idea. He's away four days at a time with his international flights anyway. But I think it's really important for me to be here for my staff, don't you think?"

"Mostly," Julia said with a slight shrug.

"What do you mean? It's part of being a leader, right? Like we talked about the other day. I feel it's important to develop my people."

"True," said Julia.

"Hmmm. I'm not sensing complete agreement. Look, I've built this business from the ground up." Redley stood up and walked over to her bookcase, reaching for a dark brown glass bottle and a tall green one. She came back to join Julia, handing her the bottles. "Here's the first beer and the first bottle of mead that came through here and not from my basement. I've done everything. From washing floors and toilets to capping bottles. We had some fun in the early days. We'd finish bottling and labeling late on a summer Saturday, then bring beers and sandwiches out on the lawn."

"Sounds like a good small business owner," observed Julia as she rotated first one bottle then the other in her hands.

"I won't ask my staff to do anything I wouldn't do. I encourage them to ask questions, to get it right. To learn from my mistakes. That's empowering them to be leaders themselves. I don't want to see anyone fail."

Julia looked at the label, a painting of a bright red mug on a rock by the water. "Who came up with your design?" she asked. "And your name? I like it. Red Tankard. It fits."

Redley smiled. "I was into the history of beer and mead. I liked how it connected me back for centuries. You know in the late 1700s most of the beer in England was made by women? It was the industrial revolution that moved beer and beer drinking into the male domain. So I liked the use of the word Tankard. My mother calls me Red, so that seemed like a natural."

"I like it," repeated Julia.

"Wait, you changed the subject. I'm sensing you have some advice you want to give me."

"You invited me for a tour, not a lesson. I don't believe in offering unsolicited advice, for a lot of reasons."

"Oh, I'm sorry. I'm not asking for free consulting. I'll hire you to coach me or something," said Redley.

Julia put the bottle down. "Redley, it's not about the money. I don't do this for the money. I've already made enough money to last me a lifetime. I do it to make a difference. I charge because in this world charging makes people value you more, and value what you say more. They pay more attention and they learn more. You don't have to pay me to just ask my opinion. Ongoing work we could talk about some other time."

"Sorry, Julia. I just wanted to be fair. I don't want to take advantage. But if you have an opinion, I'm soliciting it."

"Okay, not advice. Just an observation," said Julia. "You're a leader who's done everything. You know the business, with all its functions and details, intimately. I watched that as we toured. It's very impressive how on top of all the details you still are, even as much as you've grown!"

"I hear a but," said Redley with a wry smile.

"When you're good at something, it's easy to get caught in it, to have it become your default and not a choice. You've been doing it so long, it's easy to think no one can do without you. Then it becomes self-fulfilling. Your staff ends up coming to you for everything. You have all the answers so they keep coming."

Redley was silent for a moment. "Hence, all the interruptions."

Julia nodded. "Exactly. It's the difference between your intent and your impact. You may want to be giving them answers so they can learn quickly and won't have to make any mistakes. Unfortunately, you get them to just keep coming back for the next answer."

"I think I'm getting it, but say it a little differently. Let me make sure I get what you mean."

"You're great at solving problems. So you keep solving the problem for them. You're giving them the solution rather than making them figure out a solution, which would help them build the skills you want them to have. Plus, your reluctance to have them fail means they get reluctant to make a mistake. So they don't want to try anything without checking with you."

"I see it as training them. Teaching them to be self-sufficient."

"You may want them to be self-sufficient but that's not the result. It's almost the opposite. Look at what happened during our tour."

"Right!" Redley jumped up suddenly and started to pace the room. "I never thought about it that way. So when I give them an answer, I'm building more dependency."

"Yes, probably."

"So what should I do?"

"What do you think?" asked Julia with a smile.

"You're not going to tell me, are you?"

"I think you'd learn more by puzzling it out for yourself."

"Just like my staff would, if I let them find answers for themselves, huh? I'm always providing answers, but not questions. Questions, right?"

"Ahhh," was all Julia said.

"If I keep track of the questions instead of answering them, I might find that they fall into a pattern and if I offered some particular training, that would solve it as well," said Redley, rushing to her desk to make a note. "I get it."

There was a knock on the door and Redley's assistant stuck his head in.

"Production meeting in ten minutes, Boss Lady."

Redley nodded but kept writing. "I'll use an Excel spread sheet to track the category of questions."

"Could I stop you for a minute?" asked Julia.

Pause and Reflect

Chapter 29

R edley looked up.
"I can see you're full of ideas," said Julia, "but just one more thing."

Redley nodded, and came back to sit with Julia.

"You get an idea and move into action quickly," said Julia.

Redley tilted her head from side to side, not quite getting it.

"Okay," said Julia. "Just like now. You went immediately from realizing how you solve problems for everyone to developing a tracking and training program."

"What's wrong with that?" asked Redley, a little defensively.

"It's not about right or wrong. It's about slowing down."

"I need to move fast in this business."

"I get that. Sometimes you need to slow down to go fast. You don't have any more time in your day, do you?"

Redley shook her head and her loose knot of hair fell out of its clip. She shoved it back in annoyance.

"So you may want to use your time differently. Free yourself up from the detail. Develop your staff."

"That's what I thought I was doing," complained Redley, obviously frustrated with herself. "With a training program."

Julia explained about good problem solving process. "You become aware of a problem, just like now, then explore it, why it's happening, see if you're looking at the whole issue rather than just a symptom. Keep asking why, why is this happening? Talk to others, see how they're experiencing it. When you think you've got the whole picture, then it's on to evaluating the choices and making some plans. Then you move into action. You don't start with action."

"Right," said Redley slowly, still frowning.

"Let's get back to this specific situation. You jumped to a training program. That could be a solution, but let's think why your staff comes to you with a question or a problem."

"Because they know I'll solve it for them? Keep them from making a mistake? Maybe I shouldn't give them an answer, but make them go through the process I go through to come up with an answer?" asked Redley.

"You could try it. If you take time with them to ask questions, look at it from different angles, maybe they can start to choose an action themselves."

"Geez, Julia. That would take forever. I'd never get off the brewery floor. Training would be a lot faster."

"For some things. But how will it change your behavior? Ask yourself why the staff comes to you in the first place. You're a problem solver. A fixer. Maybe the larger issue is how to develop those same skills in your people. Training might be a part of it, but not all of the solution. Just slow yourself down to consider all angles."

"I have to think about this, Julia," said Redley.

"I like that answer. Think about it before doing anything."

"I will," said Redley slowly getting up, obviously still thinking.

Julia stood as well and shook hands with Redley. "Thank you again for a lovely tour. I'm very impressed with everything I've seen."

"You know, my staff tells me I don't ask them a lot of questions. They say I give answers. I'm wondering if that is all part of what we've been talking about," mused Redley as she walked Julia to the front lobby.

Julia just smiled. "It's something else to think about."

"Plus, I've been struggling with our productivity. Compared to my peers I've got too many employees for our production size, and our growth has been slowing. Maybe I'm holding them back."

Chapter 30

When Julia got in her little red sports car she checked for messages and saw that Cesar had called. Rather than return his call, she decided to take a chance he'd be available and drove over to the town hall. She was told he was just finishing a call, so Julia sat in the lobby area.

She refused an offer of coffee and ignored the array of magazines on the table. She looked around at the high ornate ceilings and the long row of dark portraits with dusty gold frames from an earlier era. The faint pattern of the oriental carpet was worn away in places, the wooden floor around the edges of the room was scratched and gouged. The room told the story of the town's earlier glory.

"Julia," Cesar's hearty voice called to her. "Come in. I'm so glad you're here. I need to talk with you. Sorry to keep you waiting."

Julia stood and was quickly ushered into Cesar's office.

"I need help," he said, hoisting himself from his chair. He stood for a minute with his hands braced on the imposing acre of papers covering his desk. "I don't know how…"

She looked up at him, waiting.

He sighed. "It's this reporter or blogger or whatever he calls himself. He's driving me crazy. I need to do something." He looked down at her.

She reached out and just lightly touched the chair opposite her. "Won't you sit down?" she asked.

Cesar shrugged. "Ah. Right. Can you help?"

"Perhaps. First I need to understand what you need help with."

"This reminds me of our first conversation. You kept asking me what I wanted help with. Made me be specific."

Julia nodded. "Helps us both, right? So what is it, Cesar. A way to manage your emotions? Stay out of crazy? Or do you need a strategy to manage the reporter, or at least the political fallout from the reporter's stories?"

"Both, I guess."

"Tell me more."

Cesar leaned over and pulled a copy of the article from his inbox and handed it to her while explaining the gist of it.

"What's your biggest concern, Cesar?" asked Julia after he finished. "I'm not sure I'm seeing this from your point of view."

"It's slander. Just like during my election."

"So you have a past with this person?"

Cesar nodded. "I guess you could put it that way."

"Well, what I mean is, sounds like something from the past still bothers you. You know, that could color how you see things now."

"Damn sure. Sorry, Julia. Didn't mean to curse. Look. It might help if I tell you the story. Do you have time?"

Julia looked at her watch. "It's ten thirty now. I have to be on a conference call at twelve. I'm good."

"I'll make it quick. You see, when I was running for mayor, this reporter, name of Mel Schroom if you believe it, was trying to dig up dirt. Now, my wife and I have been married since we were practically kids, I've never had an affair, never had an illegitimate child. You know the stuff politician's get caught on, that stuff just wasn't in my past."

"I'm not at all surprised, Mayor."

A quick but gracious smile lit up Cesar's face, but then he went on. "So he kept digging. Finally he wrote this story with big bold headlines. 'Mayoral Candidate Arrested on DUI While on Police Duty.' Can you imagine how I felt reading that? How my kids felt? Kelly?"

"Did he make it up?"

"There was truth to the matter, but not the way he portrayed it." Cesar went on to explain that when he was a young cop serving as dog officer he received a call while he was off duty. He had been at a wedding reception in the next town, but called in because there was a dog loose who'd bitten two people. He had been stopped on route because he had a tail light out. The officer smelled alcohol. "I was barely over the legal limit. So I got charged. But it didn't... I didn't even lose my job. I got a reprimand, which I deserved, but kept my job. I wasn't even supposed to be on call."

"Did the story cause that much of a problem in your campaign? Doesn't seem like that big a deal."

"It might have blown over but other papers picked up on the headline and it got a lot of play. Without the whole story, just seeing that headline, people in town started to question me, because I had never brought it up myself. I had to hire a lawyer. Have him collect the old evidence. Publish the evidence."

"But you won the election."

"I did win. I still felt like I'd had my reputation tarnished. And I lost a lot of sleep and spent some money."

"And now?"

Cesar took a deep breath. "It feels the same way. Look what he says here. 'The mayor didn't know what he was doing.' So what do I do?" asked Cesar.

"What are you considering?" asked Julia.

Cesar sat for a minute. "I don't know. I could put something on the town website about the criteria I used for selecting the committee. I could call the owner of the website he works for. I could... I don't know. I could call my cousins in Mexico and have him shot. No, strike that last."

Julia laughed heartily, "How about if you imagine he got hit by a bus?"

"Can I do that?" Cesar asked in surprise, then joined in her laughter.

"Why not? If it helps do something with your anger."

Cesar closed his eyes and then grinned. "Okay, now what?"

"Remember we talked about what to do when people go against you, or resist you?"

"Wish them under a bus?" asked Cesar with a chuckle. Then he sat and thought. "No. Not really. Maybe. Tell me again."

"You get curious. You wonder why are they going against you, or disagreeing. What's making them behave the way they're behaving? Where are they coming from?"

"He's trying to stir up trouble," said Cesar immediately.

"Really. Why? What's his underlying motive? How is it different from yours? What can you learn?"

"To make a name for himself?" He paused. "I don't know. I think he's just a trouble maker. A jerk."

"Maybe. But mostly, I believe that people are basically doing the best they can. Most people don't get up in the morning thinking about how they can screw up. Generally, they try to do a good enough job as they see it. As *they* see it."

"Wait a minute. There are bad people in this world. Believe me, I know," said Cesar.

"You're right. Trust me, I know that too. But even they are trying to do the best they can given their circumstances. Unfortunately their circumstances may be pure hell. Or were pure hell. If that's true for him, could be his only goal is to cause trouble. But let's put that aside for a moment. And let's put aside people who are truly twisted or evil. Let's just talk about the rest of us, okay?"

"Okay."

"So if we assume we're all doing the best we can with what we've got, when someone behaves a certain way, you start to wonder why. Try to think about it without judgment, as much as possible."

"Okay," said Cesar again.

"Why would he be digging up dirt? What way does it serve him? Is it possible he's trying to make a name for himself as an investigative journalist? Maybe he thinks that's a valuable thing to be in the world. Maybe he's trying to uncover truth."

"Humph!" said Cesar.

"Well, things have been uncovered by investigative journalists that were really important. Especially in politics. You're old enough to remember Watergate?"

"This isn't Watergate," said Cesar crankily.

"How does he know?" Julia just sat for a minute looking at Cesar. His foot was jiggling. "Look, I don't know where he's coming from. All I'm saying is you might want to try to figure it out."

"He hasn't even talked to me. How would he know anything?"

"Has he tried?" asked Julia.

Cesar grudgingly admitted that he'd turned away many attempts by Schroom to talk with him. Only his staff had actually had a conversation with the blogger.

"Whatever I say he will twist it around," said Cesar, getting up from his chair and starting to pace, rattling the change in his pocket.

"This goes back to your election?"

"You're darned right."

"Did you meet with him back then?"

"No, but…"

"Why not?"

"He wasn't one of the regular journalists in town. He was writing for this fringe hippy paper. I just figured he was digging up dirt, that he wasn't important to talk to, and I wanted nothing to do with him."

Julia just sat watching Cesar pace. He went over and looked out the window, then turned back to her.

"So you're saying I should talk to him," said Cesar, almost grinding his teeth.

"Not if you're going to chew him up and spit him out," said Julia, with a little laugh.

Cesar came back and sat down opposite Julia. He took a deep breath and let it out slowly. "Okay." He drummed his fingers on the arm of the chair for a minute. "Okay, I guess I need to talk to him." He took another deep breath and leaned toward Julia, but he grabbed onto the arms of the chair. "What do I do so I don't just blow up at him? Tell me what to say."

Pause and Reflect

Chapter 31

"How do you not blow up? Important question," agreed Julia. "You have to manage your assumptions, not just your words."

"I don't get it," said Cesar.

"If you go in assuming he's a jerk and you believe he wronged you and is going to wrong you again, that will come across. You'll be gripping the arms of the seat like you are now. If you go in assuming he's doing the best he can..." Cesar's eyebrows were one dark line across his forehead.

"His best isn't good enough for me!"

"Well, there's an assumption that will take you straight to blowing up."

"Fine, fine." Cesar shook his head as if trying to clear out the blackness. "Go on."

"Okay, if you go in assuming he's doing the best he can even if his best isn't good enough for you. If you go in with some optimism and curiosity, you'll have a different interaction. Trust me on this."

Cesar considered her words. He tipped his head and repeated them. "Optimism and curiosity. Optimism that we can work things out? That he's not a jerk or a toad? That he'll listen?"

"Yes. All of that. Optimism that he's a human being just like you, trying to get along in the world. That you'll come out having learned something."

"But what if he's just trying to ruin me?"

"You know you'll figure out what to do if, in fact, he turns out to be intent on ruining you, which I certainly hope isn't true. Until you know, put that thought aside and explore what else might be going on for him."

Cesar tapped his fingers lightly on his knee. "Maybe I could do that."

"If you go in with those assumptions inside you, you'll act differently. You can't help it. It happens from the inside out.

He'll respond differently to it. Remember that time when I was teaching during your meeting and you didn't like it? Remember how you said you felt when I didn't defend myself? I was assuming you had good reason to respond as you did and I was trying to see it from your point of view. You felt that and reacted differently, right?"

"I hear you. It makes sense. Once again, your wisdom is appreciated."

"Experience brings wisdom."

"Not for everyone," said Cesar.

"True. Not for everyone," agreed Julia.

"I'll have my aide set up a call with him."

"Well...." Julia hesitated.

"No? I thought you were encouraging me to get in touch with him."

Chapter 32

"Set up a call with Schroom?" asked Julia. "Did you say a call because you think it's the best way, or because it's your default choice?"

"Ahhh," said Cesar, nodding his head slightly. He tapped his fingers on the arm of the chair then shrugged. "My default choice. Now that you're making me pay attention, I think a face-to-face meeting would be a better strategy. I could have him come in. No wait. I could offer to go see him." Cesar grinned. "That would certainly throw him off base." He put up his hands and laughed. "Sorry. I'm going to try to approach this with optimism and thinking the best."

"With any meeting where there are differences, or potential conflict, making good contact, a real connection, is critical. And making good contact is easier in person," urged Julia. "You get to watch his expressions, his body language and he gets to watch yours. You get to sense one another."

"Sort of like dogs sniffing one another?" Cesar said with a smirk.

"Don't laugh. Yes, exactly. Well, not exactly, but sort of. We put out a kind of…. I don't know what word you'd prefer, I call it presence, in all sorts of subtle ways that we pick up on in one another."

"Isn't that what you were saying he'd pick up on if I went in assuming he was a jerk?"

"Sure, of course. Assumptions are a big part of presence, how you impact people."

"What else should I pay attention to?" asked Cesar.

"You know there was this wonderful book I read some years ago by a woman brain researcher who had a stroke. Jill Bolte Taylor. She wrote all about her experience in this impaired state. It was fascinating. One thing that struck me was how much the approach and attitude of her caregivers impacted her when her brain was mostly shut down. She was incredibly sensitive to it, maybe because the normal filters we all have when our brain is working were down. Anyway she had a sign put up on her door—something like 'Be careful of the energy you bring into this room.'"

"I guess that makes sense. I remember having my knee replacement and one particular nurse was in such a hurry. She'd act like my boss, rush in, tell me what to do, rush around, and rush out. It drove me crazy."

"So another thing you could think about is how you want to set up the hierarchy."

"What does that mean?" asked Cesar.

"Well, you mentioned dogs before. It's like top dog, underdog."

"I don't get your drift. How does that play in here?"

"Here's an example. If you invite him here to your office and sit behind your desk, it gives you an immediate power advantage. That's not to say he doesn't have power either. But think about it. You're older. You're the mayor. You're here supported by all the trappings of your office. If you want to play that card, sit behind your desk. If not, at least come around and sit next to him, in one of these desk chairs like you are now."

"Or I could go see him…" said Cesar, as sort of a question.

"Right. Earlier you mentioned going to see him. That would be a choice where you were intentionally creating a more balanced hierarchy. It depends on how you want to come across. What impact you want to make."

"Something else to think about."

"Whatever you do, be intentional. Do it with choice and awareness of the impact on him, instead of by default. Pay attention to not just what you want to say but how you want to come across. Big tough powerful mayor? Curious person who cares about this town? How do you want him to see you?"

"Now that you say that, I suppose it's not just true for him. It plays out in terms of my employees, my constituents."

"Absolutely! Of course. Especially in your role. Also because of your size. You're a big man. You have a big presence in a room. You can easily be intimidating."

"Wait a minute, Julia. I could say the same for you. You're a tiny woman and you have a surprisingly big presence, too."

"I do. I know I do." She chuckled. "People don't expect it."

Cesar laughed. "We have to watch our assumptions, right?"

"Let's get back to you," Julia said, nodding. "Just be thinking about your intent and your impact. Be thinking about really connecting with him as a person before you get down to business, you know? Again, it's what you'd probably do with one of your voters. You'd ask about them, their families, find some common ground first, wouldn't you?"

"Sure I would. Do it all the time."

"There you go. You just do the same with this blog person. I sometimes call it starting with the intimate connection."

"I'll remember with that title. That's rather provocative, isn't it?"

"It gets people's attention. What I mean is intimate as in relational, building a relationship. It's a foundation. Then move on to the business, the strategic part of the conversation. I talked with Fletcher about this but you might not have been in the room. You're more natural at building connections but you'll have to be intentional this time. Connection before action."

"I will. I will, indeed," Cesar said as he stood up. "You've given me a lot to think about here. Thank you. I'll try some of these ideas right away."

"You're a good man, Cesar. A good leader. You're willing to be open. To learn. To try something new."

"Come on," said Cesar, his face reddening. "I'll walk you out."

"Wait a minute. Slow down. Take in the feedback. It's not true of all leaders."

He put his hand to his heart and paused. "I hear you. Thank you, Julia." He made a little bow. "There. Is that better?"

She laughed. "Sort of."

Pause and Reflect

Chapter 33

S everal days later, the Blue Ribbon Committee gathered in the town hall conference room. Because Mel Schroom had been out of town, the mayor hadn't been able to contact him, but the casino rumor seemed to be gaining momentum. All four of them felt the urgency to get something to the townspeople.

"All right, this brings us back to the issue of a survey. We're all in agreement we need to go out to the town somehow, right?" asked Cesar.

"Yes, but we haven't agreed on what happens with the results, Chief," warned Redley.

"I know," said Cesar. "Let's begin with that. I'm all about paying attention to the will of the people, you know that. That's my job. But that said, I'll try to stay open. Let's go back to what Fletcher was saying last time. Remind us, Fletcher."

"I think the leader is fully accountable," said Fletcher. "So we should make the final decision."

"A leader is," said Mark. "But we're not the leaders of this town. We're just an appointed committee."

"Wait a minute," said Redley. "This doesn't feel right. Before we get too far, what were those three rules again from the birds? I know the first was asking questions, but…"

"Take your share of time," said Mark.

"And responsibility," said Cesar.

"Anyone remember the last one?" asked Redley. "Don't tell us, Julia."

"Why shouldn't she tell us?" asked Mark.

"We'll learn more if we do it ourselves," said Redley, then stopped. She repeated herself. "We'll learn more if we do it ourselves. Right?" she said, turning to Julia. "That's what you're trying to get me to understand?"

Julia just smiled.

"What's she talking about?" asked Fletcher, dryly.

Redley kicked off her high heels and tucked her jean clad legs up under her. "Never mind. What's the third rule. Think!"

"Something about refocusing your lens," said Fletcher.

"Right," said Mark. "Big picture and details. Yourself and others. So if I go out to the big picture, ultimately, whose responsibility really is this?"

"I guess mine," said Cesar, "since I'm the only one of us that's been elected. But I chose you to represent the town."

"Okay, but is it ours or is it the townspeople's? Shouldn't they be the ultimate deciders?" Mark addressed not just Cesar but the whole group.

Fletcher frowned. "I think of leadership as including having a vision of where I need to take my organization. I look for input, yes, but I determine the course. Isn't that the role of the leader, Julia?"

She shrugged slightly. "Yes and no. I've read a lot about this question of what is the role of the leader. Sometimes I see it one way, then I get curious again. At one point I saw it as all about presence, the big charisma."

"And now?" prompted Redley.

"I don't care much about charisma, although presence, as in being fully present, has something to do with it. It's got to be a more inclusive process," said Julia. "There's too much facing leaders today to do it alone. Too many unknowns. Too much coming at them. I don't like the idea of the leader as hero anymore. Especially not in these complex times."

"But what about establishing the vision?" asked Fletcher. "Isn't that my ultimate responsibility?"

"Wait a minute, do you really have the ultimate responsibility?" Mark asked Fletcher. "Don't you have a board of directors?"

"Of course!" Fletcher responded quickly. "So, in that sense, you're right. They're accountable. Usually, though, they don't have enough day-to-day knowledge to really know what course to set. I propose the direction. Don't get me wrong. I'm open to input. From my staff and from the directors.

What about you, Redley. Don't you set the course at Red Tankard? You're the sole owner, after all."

"Definitely," said Redley. "I think if people don't know where we're going they won't know how to take us there. I guess I think more about the fact that as a leader I need to be out front. I need to be out ahead, thinking further ahead than anyone else. I need to see around the bend so when everyone approaches it they don't go shooting off the side of the road. Although Julia's got me thinking about my leadership. Maybe I'll have a different answer next time you ask. What about you, Mark?"

"Hey, look. Me? Leadership? I learned about leadership in medical school. The doctor was king. Then in residency, the chief resident was king. When I finished my training, all of a sudden I was king of my practice and frankly, at that time, I still didn't know my ass from my elbow, except in an anatomical way. I didn't have any idea how to manage staff." He shrugged. "I did the best I could. Now my world is pretty much turned upside down. The doctor isn't king. I guess the insurance companies are. Even the patients. They come in with their print outs from Google searches and their lists of questions. They expect to collaborate in their own treatment. Which is good. Mostly. There are times, though, when I just need to insist on what I think is best."

"This is interesting, folks," said Cesar, "but it's not moving us toward a decision. What should we do with this survey? Julia do you have an opinion?"

"I'm hearing that you're all pretty much on the same page," she said. "You all think you have a responsibility to make the final decision but you have to take the town vote into your consideration as part of the data you use to make the decision. Right?"

"You got that from this discussion?" asked Cesar in surprise. "Okay. Mark? Fletcher? Redley? Do you agree?"

"I think she's right," said Mark. "I know I was the one pushing to let the town decide, but I guess you've all convinced me that we should get their opinion, but use it as part of our decision, not as the decider itself."

Fletcher and Redley nodded.

"Okay then," said Cesar. "I can live with that. Let's just make sure the voters all know that."

Redley nodded. "I'll put it right at the top of the survey. Non-binding."

"Fine. Then let's talk about the next steps," said Cesar. "Any ideas?"

Chapter 34

"Let's talk about how to involve people more than just in an online survey," said Mark. "Get them engaged. We need to be out letting them ask questions. They can't make an informed choice on the survey without a chance to hear about the choices."

"We need to be visible," agreed Redley. "It needs to be interactive, like some meetings for the people to ask us questions in person."

"That's an excellent idea," said Mark. "That's what we need to do."

They agreed to three evening meetings and three breakfast meetings, just for the purposes of sharing information with anyone and everyone who might be interested.

"Make sure to leave time for questions," said Redley. "But what if they don't say anything? How do we get them to ask questions, Julia?"

Julia smiled. "They probably will, but here's what I do. I ask 'what questions do you have,' not 'do you have any questions?' Then be prepared to wait quietly. Don't cut off the silence too soon."

As they planned the schedule for the six meetings, the mayor turned to Julia.

"These meetings have to be good. They have to capture people's attention and get them engaged," said Cesar. "Any ideas, Julia?"

"You talked about natural cycles," said Mark, remembering.

"Good beginning, middles, and ends," added Redley.

Julia nodded. "The natural rhythm of how work gets done. It applies to these meetings."

"Go over it again," asked Cesar.

"You're asking me to lecture?" said Julia, tilting her head and raising one eyebrow.

Cesar laughed and winked at her. "Yes, Julia. Lecture away. I won't complain a bit."

"I think about it like this," began Julia as she stood up and walked slowly toward the flip chart. "The world moves in cycles, you know? Like day and night. Spring, summer, fall, winter."

She looked around and everyone was nodding. "I'll show you a more detailed version of when we talked about good beginnings and endings. The same basic concept as that change process we talked about, Mark."

"It's like a mountain and we're leading a hike," said Mark.

"I don't hike," said Fletcher quickly.

"You like data, Fletcher, and models, right?" asked Julia. He nodded.

She got up and went to the flip chart. "This is a model of how work gets done." She drew a big L. "The vertical line is energy and the horizontal line is time." Then she drew a bell curve.

"And that thing that looks like a mountain?" asked Cesar.

"Think of this as the cycle of your meeting," she said. At the left low side she wrote the word *Awareness*. "So let's start at the beginning of the meeting, with awareness. The good beginning, remember? A really good beginning gets people connected, to each other and really to themselves."

"We could have a meet and greet with food at the beginning," said Redley. "Be outside shaking hands, welcoming people, giving them nametags, introducing them to one another."

"That's a good idea," said Mark. "We could also make sure we offer up something personal when we introduce ourselves to the audience."

"Could we ask them to say anything?" asked Cesar.

"That could take a long time," said Fletcher.

"Any ideas, Julia?" asked Cesar.

"With large groups," Julia explained, "I might get them standing up or raising their hands in response to different questions. Like how many people have lived here more than ten years?"

"How about how many people think they get enough exercise?" said Mark.

"Or how many people have ever wanted to own their own business?" added Redley.

"Who listens to classical music?" said Fletcher.

Cesar laughed. "We'll ask them all," he said, taking quick notes. "What next, Julia?"

Julia turned to the flip chart and halfway up the left side of the curve she wrote the word *Engagement*. "The next phase is about increasing awareness with the issue. Why are we together, why does it matter, why should we be doing anything? It's getting people engaged with the problem. Building their focus, their interest and involvement."

"So we present the agenda," said Fletcher. "Highlight the issues we're trying to solve."

"How about pictures of downtown when it was vibrant and alive, twenty years ago," offered Mark.

"Could we pair them with pictures taken from the same place right now?" asked Redley.

"I'll have my staff work on that. I know we have archives that will help," said Cesar.

"What about a chart of the changing population data?" asked Fletcher.

"Let's make it a bar graph with images of people on it," offered Redley. "That will resonate more."

They each threw in a few more ideas.

"The top of the curve, or the mountain if that's what you're calling it, is the 'what.' What is it that you're going to do. Mobilization, I call it." Julia winked at the mayor, and wrote the word at the top of the curve. "This is what I was explaining the other week. You're at the top of the mountain and you look all around. It's about examining what's going on and testing the potential choices, the conditions. Lets people get into the details. It's really important people get to ask all their questions here. This stage often gets rushed."

"I don't get this mobilization thing," said Redley. "Or at least how it applies here.

"I think I do," said Fletcher. "This is the data phase."

"This is where we present all three plans?" asked Mark.

"Yes," said Julia. "Exactly. This phase is all about collecting and analyzing the data and planning. That's what you want to allow the folks at the meeting to do. With plenty of time for people to ask questions. Make it interactive. Don't just talk at them constantly. Get them talking, with their neighbor, perhaps, or in groups of four or five. Let them talk before you go on to the next plan. You can ask the groups to each come up with a question. That helps people get over their reticence to talk in public."

"Great idea," said Cesar. "I like that. Get people talking!"

"We can give them copies of the plans so they'll have something to look at as they talk," said Fletcher.

"What next, Julia?" asked Mark.

She wrote the word *Action* halfway down the right side of the curve. "This is where implementation occurs. The how. How are we going to solve this problem?"

"I don't get it," said Mark. "Isn't that the plans we've just presented?"

"In a way," said Julia. "What I mean is, how should they act on the issue? From this meeting? How do they do something?"

Mark shook his head.

"We want them to be forming an opinion for the survey," said Redley quickly. "We want them to know about the survey. We want them to fill out the survey."

"Either online or at the town hall or libraries," added Fletcher.

"That sounds right," said Cesar.

Julia nodded.

"So," said Redley thoughtfully, "in this meeting the action is creating readiness to choose which plan they like best. They need to know what we'll do with their choice. How the grant process will be completed. Maybe your opinion on the casino rumor, Chief. All the next steps."

"Not that casino. Not that," said Cesar with finality.

"It's not within our purview or our control," said Fletcher.

"Are we done then?" Mark asked Julia. "Is that the end?"

She shook her head and wrote the word *Evaluation* at the bottom of the right side of the curve. "The last phase is the evaluation phase. Too often we skip it because we run out of time and/or energy. But it's important. Before you finish up, make sure everyone's with you. It's that good ending we talked about weeks ago. In this case, how did they feel about the meeting? Do they understand what they need to do? You sometimes ask for feedback about the meeting."

"We should do that, especially because we're going to have more than one meeting," said Cesar.

"Good," said Julia. "So ask how did they like the format? How could it be better? Evaluation is the last phase of the process." On her diagram under the horizontal line she wrote three words, *Why, What, How* to finish the diagram.

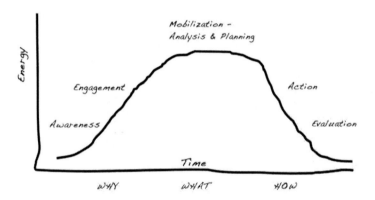

"You start out with *why*," continued Julia, "building awareness why you are meeting, which moves you into the *what*. What's the data and choices? What will you consider doing? Then once you've got that figured out you have to move to take action—the *how*—getting it done and assessing how well you did it."

"This diagram does remind me of the change process," said Mark.

"And the advice you gave me about meeting with Schroom?" asked Cesar.

"Exactly," said Julia. "Micros and macros. It could be a phone conversation, a small team meeting, a personal change process like buying a new car or losing weight, or a major change process like trying to improve a town. It applies to the meetings you'll have but also to the whole process of your grant application."

"I like the metaphor of the mountain," said Redley. "It makes sense. When you climb a mountain the view changes at each point. Plus it's harder to go up than to go down. The important thing is to notice where you are."

"Right," said Julia. "Don't lose your awareness."

Fletcher sighed. "Awareness again."

Cesar smiled. "This is the fun part, Fletcher! Come on. Out talking with people, convincing them to be active in participating. This will be great."

"Spoken like a true politician," said Fletcher wryly.

"Which we're not," said Mark. "You're used to this, Mayor. I'm not a public speaker and I feel awkward about presenting to townspeople. What could make it easier, Julia?"

Chapter 35

"What do you want help with?" Julia asked Mark.

He shrugged. "I don't know. I mean, we talked about how to structure the meetings. What about how we make a good impression in a public meeting?"

Fletcher and Redley both leaned forward in their chairs. "I could use that," said Redley. "I do a lot of sales presentations, but this is different. More formal."

"Is it?" asked Julia. "Maybe not so different. The audience is just bigger. Tell me what you do in a sales presentation."

"Well...." Redley thought for a minute. "Of course it's different every time." She hesitated. "I can't describe it."

"Just take us through what you're thinking about, the general steps you go through, what you try to accomplish," said Julia.

"I guess I start with getting to know the person, you know, we chit chat a bit. I use that time to get a feel for their personality and their way of doing business." Redley looked up at the ceiling for a minute, thinking. "We start talking about their current purchasing, what works for them, what doesn't work for them."

"Okay. What about your demeanor? Do you give any thought to how you want to come across?"

"Hmmm. I certainly prepare myself in advance. I used to worry about it a lot because I knew I had to build quick credibility. I'd plan out what to wear, you know, how formal or informal, depending on who I was meeting with. Like Fletcher, putting on his jacket for Mark but not for me."

"Please, Redley," said Fletcher. "I'll put my jacket on for you next time if you want. After all, it says nothing about the respect I have for you."

"Don't change anything," she said. "I like the more informal, personal approach, so the fact you don't bother with your jacket says you know me."

Julia asked what other things Redley thought about in advance.

Redley described her sales research, her examination of the company's online presence, website, reviews and news releases. "It helps me to start seeing things from their point of view."

"We should think about the audience then, how they'll be feeling when they arrive," said Mark.

Julia nodded.

Redley went on to talk about other ways she used her research. "The information helps clear my mind of any wrong assumptions I might hold about them."

"Say more about assumptions," said Fletcher. "What do you mean?"

"Oh, preconceived notions that may or may not be right. Their level of success, or their type of clientele. Speaking of assumptions, I don't do this as much, but I used to have to pay close attention to my assumption about myself—that I wasn't experienced enough, or my company wasn't big enough for them, or that the person I was meeting was somehow better than me. That totally got in my way. Now, I prepare by remembering how proud I am of my products and services and how they'll benefit from doing business with us."

"So how can you use Redley's sales process at these community meetings?" asked Julia. "Any ideas?"

"That assumption thing stood out for me," said Mark. "I was already assuming I can't do this. I'll prepare by focusing on my confidence about the benefits of a community center."

"Important idea, Mark," said Julia, nodding. "Your presence starts from what's going on inside your head and your heart. There's some research showing that the actual words you use have less impact than what your body language and facial expressions communicate, especially when they're in conflict. And your body often gives away what's in your head and heart. What about you, Fletcher? How do you prepare?"

He sighed. "I don't know. Let's see. I make notes. A complete outline of the points I want to cover," said Fletcher.

"The one thing with notes I wouldn't do is read an actual word-for-word speech. I learned that in my first week of campaigning," said Cesar. "Boy, did I bomb! I never did that again."

"What about writing it out and memorizing it?" asked Mark.

"That will take away from your contact with the audience, unless you've got a lot of experience," said Julia. "Your mind ends up focusing on remembering the words rather than staying aware of connecting with the people in front of you."

"Yeah," said Redley. "We're not actors, after all. And let's be careful about too much PowerPoint, too," said Redley. "I hate those slides covered with words that are too tiny for me to read so the presenter feels they have to read them to me. Totally boring."

"What else?" asked Mark. "What else should we be thinking about?"

"Go back to Redley's sales process," suggested Julia. "What do you do next, Redley?"

"Let's see. If I felt the person was ready, I'd describe my company and our products. I pay a lot of attention to pace—how fast or slow I have to go. I watch them for confusion, for questions."

"I do that in my regular constituent meetings," said the mayor.

"Pacing is one of the biggest mistakes people make," said Julia, "When people are nervous they often speed up. It's a combination of adrenalin moving them along and also their desire to get it over with in a hurry."

"That will be me," said Mark, raising his hand and laughing.

"So what can you do?" asked Julia.

"Practice?" asked Mark.

"Yes…. The more comfortable you get with your content, the better, so you can concentrate on the audience and their reactions. If you're aware of the tendency to rush, you could bring an environmental cue to slow down."

"What's an environmental cue?" asked the mayor curiously.

"Something in the environment that helps you remember, like the old string around the finger. It could be something Mark brings to the podium, like a special water bottle. He might make red marks here and there on his notes to remind him to slow down."

"Hmmmm," said Mark. "I can do that. I think the water bottle would work for me. Maybe I'll put a rubber band around it."

"So Redley, how do you finish up?" asked Julia.

"Well, I make sure I've summarized my main points, what I think was important to them. Then I ask for the business, always. Or for an appropriate next step if they aren't ready to buy. A visit to the brewery. A call to another client for a testimonial."

"So what would that mean in these presentations?" asked Julia.

"We need to summarize the data we've offered," said Fletcher. "The cogent information and completing the survey."

Julia nodded. "Absolutely. Think about what's the most important thing for them to remember."

"But we shouldn't race through it," said Mark.

Julia nodded. "Is there anything else you think about, Cesar, when you make a speech? You're the expert on this."

"I'm no expert, so I can always use a few tips," said Cesar. "The one thing you didn't talk about isn't probably an issue in a sales presentation. I have to pay attention to standing still or walking around slowly. I used to rock back and forth as I talked, or pace, or put my hand in my pocket and jiggle my change."

"You still do that," said Redley, chuckling.

"But not on stage," said Cesar. "Kelly, my wife, said it drove her crazy. She made me practice talking while standing still in front of a mirror at home. Also posture. I tend to hunch forward if I'm upset or not quite confident about the topic I'm discussing. I have to remind myself to straighten up."

Everyone instinctively readjusted themselves in their seats. "One more thing," added Cesar. "Sounds kind of corny, but something my wife told me she did helped me the most early on when I was new to being up there without a uniform. She told me she concentrates on caring about the audience."

"I like that," said Mark. Redley nodded.

"All these things we're talking about impact your presence," said Julia. "You won't remember everything so pick one thing to concentrate on, what you think will make the most difference for you," advised Julia.

They finished up by summarizing what they'd decided and agreed to arrive thirty minutes early the night of the first meeting, at the high school auditorium.

As they walked out together, Mark caught up with Julia. "I'm still having some issues with the changes at my clinic. Can you come by tomorrow?"

Pause and Reflect

Chapter 36

The weather had turned clear but colder when Julia arrived at Mark's clinic the next day. She was wearing a pale blond coat that matched her hair and brown leather boots. They walked to the staff kitchen together. Mark showed Julia where everything was to prepare her coffee but there were no more cups. He opened the door to the storeroom, and before he could do anything the wiry haired, brown and black dog with big white spots of fur jumped up and ran toward Julia.

"Down, Muldoon," yelled Mark. "Stop!"

The dog was already jumping up, his paws leaving dusty footprints on Julia's coat. Julia was so short he came up to her shoulders. She tried unsuccessfully to hold him away.

"Down, you stupid mutt," Mark yelled again, his hand closing around the dog's collar. He pulled him off Julia. "I'm so sorry." Mark dragged the dog toward the storeroom. "Come!" But Muldoon wasn't having any part of it. Finally Mark stretched out one hand and reached into a bucket on the end of the counter. He came up with a dog biscuit. "Treat?" With that enticement he was able to get the dog into the store room and shut the door.

"I'm so sorry, Julia," he said again.

She laughed and brushed off her coat. "No real harm done."

"I bring him to work when I know I'm going to have a long day but never into the clinic, even after everyone's left. Some of my patients have dog allergies."

They got their coffee and Mark brought her through the offices and upstairs, introducing her to his medical staff on the way.

"This is my business office. It's kind of messy," said Mark, moving some piles of papers. "My clinic manager used to keep it very organized. She'd be horrified to see it."

They sat down at a small round table that Mark cleared off. He put a box of pastries on the table.

"I've been working on the things we talked about before," he said, "but I'm still having problems," Mark said.

"Did you get that article I sent?" asked Julia.

Mark looked a little sheepish and admitted he'd received it but hadn't had time to read it.

"Of course you didn't," said Julia, and Mark's expression cleared. "I just wanted to make sure you'd gotten it. You're so busy. Do you think you'll get to read it or should I just talk about it?"

"No, I'll read it."

"Really, Mark," said Julia "Is that true? Will you read it?"

"I said I would," said Mark, his voice verging on impatient.

"But you probably won't have time," objected Julia.

"I have to read medical journals. I'm sure I'll get to this."

"Why bother?" asked Julia calmly. "Why not just say no?"

"Well, you went to the trouble of sending it," said Mark, picking up a pastry, then putting it down on a napkin in front of him. "Seems rude to say no."

"That doesn't mean you need to read it. It's not rude to say no if you're too busy." He shrugged and avoided eye contact. Julia looked at him steadily as she sipped her coffee. "Mark, do you ever say no?"

He tilted his head to one side, then the other. "Mostly not," he said. They both laughed. "I like to be a nice guy. That's important, right?"

"Indeed. As long as it doesn't get in your way. Did you like receiving the article, Mark?"

"Well…"

"Come on, really, what did you feel when you saw it in your inbox?"

Mark was silent. He finished his bite then sipped some coffee. Finally he spoke. "Truthfully? I was annoyed to see it there. Another something to do that I don't have time for."

"That's good to know. I'm glad you told me," said Julia. "Why?"

"So I won't send anything else you don't want. You could have told me that when I first mentioned it. I would have trusted you more."

"What do you mean?"

"If I know you are willing to say no, I can believe you when you say yes. I trust you'll say what you mean."

"I suppose," said Mark, sounding doubtful.

"Why do you think you don't like to say no?"

"That's easy. My dad was a Marine. We never said no to him. Never. We kept moving from school to school and it was always easier not to say no there, too. I don't like conflict. I don't like to hurt people. Then in medical school, and in residency, who gets to say no? You just provide what they want."

"Do you trust when someone always says yes to you? Or do you start to wonder?"

He shook his head. "I don't know. I guess I've never thought about it. I suppose I like it."

"Oh, come on," said Julia. "Really? Think about it. Think back to someone you know, or knew in the past, who always said yes. Always agreed with you. Always went along with whatever you wanted."

"Okay. When you put it like that. I dated someone like that. Her name was Moonacuss. What a silly name. Her parents named her after the place they conceived her. She would never say no. Never gave an opinion. Whatever I suggested we do, she'd say yes. Whatever I suggested to eat, she'd order. It was awful."

"Maybe you're not such a nice guy," said Julia.

Mark frowned. "What do you mean?"

"I mean it as a compliment. You don't want someone to always say yes. That's a good thing, right?"

"Yes, I guess so."

"Do you really think that, or do you just not want to disagree?"

Mark took a deep breath, his lips tight together.

"You're doing it again," said Julia. At that they both laughed. "All I'm trying to show you is that saying what you think can make it easier for you and for those around you. Should you say everything? Of course not. For you, however, getting along with people and avoiding conflict is well-developed. You do it without thinking. Plus, it's served you well, right?"

"Sure," said Mark. "Med school. My career. My patient relationships. My staff, until now."

"Of course. It's an important skill to be able to get along. It's just that you try to do it all the time. It's your default, regardless of the situation."

"That's why some of my staff is ignoring me? Even after I've made sure they understand why, and they know how, and I've answered all their questions? They don't believe I'll make them do it?"

"What do you think?"

"Probably," said Mark, finally. "I get what you mean, but I don't know that I can do it differently."

"People make all kinds of changes to their behavior, Mark. It takes paying attention and it takes practice. Lots of little steps. You ask patients to make changes, right?"

"Like weight loss. Lifestyle changes, exercise, that sort of thing."

"Exactly, weight loss is a great example. It's about making different choices, not totally giving up food. I don't want you to give up being a nice guy and become some jerk who never gets along. That would be awful. It's not about stopping what you do well, it's about expanding your range so it's not your only choice."

"I'll have to give that some thought. But, as usual, I'm late. I've got to get back to my patients. What should I be thinking about?"

"Setting expectations. Holding people to them. Telling them 'No, you can't avoid this.'"

Mark nodded. "That used to be my manager's role."

"Now you get to practice," said Julia crisply. "Think of it as an experiment. You know, Mark, there's a Thurber line that's something like, 'You might as well fall flat on your face as lean over too far backwards.'"

Mark smiled ruefully. "So if I try and fail and fall on my face I'll still be better off than I am now?"

Julia smiled back and nodded. "That's the gist of it. You can tell me how you're doing at the first community meeting."

Pause and Reflect

Chapter 37

The first of the town meetings went well with an engaged and supportive audience until the end. Just before they finished a young man with short brown hair and heavy black glasses wearing a leather jacket stood up with a question about the casino rumor. The mayor answered.

"No one at town hall has been approached by any casino developer or any partnership. Not my office. The town planning department and the building department have not received any plans or even any inquiries about zoning or set backs or by-laws. Given that there has been no action, we have to assume this is no more than a rumor, until we have evidence otherwise."

"Shouldn't you be looking at other options for this site, especially a job creator like a casino, in case the grant doesn't get funded, regardless of which choice you make?" the man responded.

"We're quite confident that a good proposal will win us these funds," said the mayor.

"But what if it doesn't?" the man challenged.

Red suffused the mayor's face. He took a deep breath and looked back toward where Julia was sitting, although he couldn't see her in the darkness at the back of the auditorium. "Well, you ask a good question. I wonder if you have any other ideas in mind?"

"I don't, but I think you should be looking at that. If you haven't heard from the casino developer, maybe you should go out and look for one. Something that would create lots of jobs. That's what we need," said the man in the audience, looking around at the people sitting near him. "Right? Don't we?" There were head nods throughout the audience.

"You're absolutely right in your statement that this town needs jobs," responded the mayor. "If you come up with any specific ideas I'll be curious to hear them. In the meantime, you've heard three exciting proposals. If and when the grant funding comes through for any of these proposals, jobs will immediately be created and the beneficial effects on the attractiveness of the town will create further opportunities. However, if the grant funding does not come through, we will certainly have to look for private funding and/or private development ideas. I think we're out of time here but the committee will stay here for a few minutes to have further conversation, and I invite anyone to come see me at town hall. Thank you all for coming and we look forward to the feedback you'll provide us by completing the electronic survey."

There was a smattering of applause and people stood up and started to exit the auditorium. Some stood talking in small groups.

"Who was that?" Mark asked Cesar as they gathered together on the stage after most of the audience had left.

"I don't know. Let's see if anyone else knows." Cesar went down the side stairs and over to where several of his staff stood chatting. He talked to them briefly, and looked startled at what they said. As he came back up on stage to join the committee members, his expression had turned to annoyance.

"That was Mel Schroom, the news blogger who's been after me… really after us," he said to the other three.

They all turned and looked to the place where the man in the leather jacket had been sitting. He was gone.

By that time, Julia had made her way to the stage. "You all did very well," she said.

"Until that last bit," said Cesar.

"That was fine," said Julia. "You handled it well."

Cesar sighed. "That was the reporter blogger guy. Mel Schroom. The one I've been trying to reach who's been out of town. Obviously, he's back."

"Ahhh," said Julia. "Okay, we can come back to that, but it might makes sense to do a quick review of this meeting first."

"Right," said Cesar. "Can we all sit for about ten minutes?"

"Awww," said Redley. "Do we have to? My feet hurt and I'm beat. Hungry, too. Can't we do it after tomorrow's meeting?"

"I know," said Julia. "Trouble is if you wait it's harder to remember and find the time. This is exactly what I meant about how easy it is to skip the evaluation part of the cycle. Believe me, it will take less time right now when it's fresh on your minds."

"Of course. Let's go over what we'd do differently next time." said Cesar as the others nodded. They pulled their chairs together and got one for Julia from the wings of the stage. Redley kicked off her high heels and massaged her left foot.

"I'd suggest a different question to start with," said Julia. "Before we get to what to do differently, it's important to look at what you liked. I think it will help, Mayor."

He nodded.

"So what were you pleased with? Each of you," Julia said as she looked from face to face.

"Ladies first," said Cesar, looking at Redley.

"Okay. Let me see," she said, tucking her foot under her. "I think we each had good presence, as Julia would say. I think we all had credible presentations on our proposals. We certainly kept the audience's attention. No one rushed. I liked that we were all positive, no sniping at each other's ideas. And we had good visuals."

Everyone nodded.

"What about you, Fletcher?" asked the mayor. "You've been to lots of town meetings. What did you think?"

"I think Redley's right. I also think you started us well, Mayor, giving the grant information, with the context of the data, and setting up the rest of the meeting," said Fletcher. "What I believe Julia called framing."

Cesar nodded. "Thank you. How about you, Mark?"

"I really enjoyed meeting people as they walked in. That worked well and it definitely helped me. I saw people I haven't seen in a long time and met several new folks. I also liked the way we engaged people, got them talking and asking questions right off the bat. And I'm really, really pleased that the first one is over!"

They all laughed.

"So what would we want to do differently next time?" asked Cesar.

"Just a minute," slowed Julia. "What are you pleased with, Mayor?"

He hemmed and hawed. "I'm having trouble getting past the end. That bit with the toadstool." When others questioned, he sheepishly told them about his name for the blogger. "That isn't respectful, making fun of his name. I know. I'm sorry. He's a constituent, too."

"You know," said Julia, "When people get to us, it's something to pay attention to. Why is this person such a trigger for you?"

"I don't know! I hate the fact that he's just so willing to shoot his mouth off! Whether here or on that damn blog of his."

"So, maybe it's because you don't get to do that," offered Redley. "You know? Maybe he gets to you because you can't just speak without considering the consequences. That's been true for you for many years, hasn't it?"

"Sure. As a cop. Certainly as mayor."

"So there you go," said Redley. "Interesting."

"It may or may not be that simple," said Julia gently. "But I only mention it because sometimes I know I can get stuck reacting to people in a certain way. Exploring why sometimes helps me have a bit more choice about it."

Cesar took a deep breath and smoothed his mustache with his hands. "Okay. I'm going to take Julia's point of view and assume he's doing the best he can. That he believes this is important for the town. He's right, I guess. So what am I pleased with? Okay. That you were each so well prepared and on point. I'm also really pleased I didn't get angry with him in the moment. That I was able to stay curious."

"I like that we started with the good stuff," said Redley. "It makes me proud of our work."

"That's very important," agreed Julia. The others nodded. "Now, if you want, Mayor, you can ask your question about improvements for next time."

"I'd like us to bring the casino issue in ourselves," said Cesar, "and not wait for Schroom to do it. I've got to find out more about that somehow. Maybe if I can finally meet with him, he can tell me who to talk to."

"Speaking just for myself," said Mark, "I think I still need to go slower, don't you think?"

They all nodded.

"I think we should give the handouts out at the beginning rather than have them on the tables for people to take at the end," said Fletcher. "I know I said to wait because they'd be flipping pages while we talked and it would be noisy, but I've changed my mind. They could look along, or even look over the data before we present. I think that would help them ask more questions," said Fletcher.

"Yeah, I agree," said Redley. "I looked out at the faces and thought they looked confused at times."

"Good. Anything else?" asked Julia.

They were all silent. "What did you notice, Julia?" asked Cesar.

"You all did well, in all the ways you've already said. The only thing I'd say is that because your presentations were so thorough you may have had to rush the ending. Perhaps you were distracted by the casino question."

"Right," said Redley. "We could spend a little more time explaining the online survey process."

"Also on asking them if they had any suggestions to improve the next meeting," suggested Mark.

"But, we were out of time," Cesar said, sounding slightly defensive.

"You were," agreed Julia.

Cesar frowned, then he resettled himself in his chair and took a deep breath. "Never mind. I know I hate negative feedback. I'm trying here." He looked at Julia. "I am. I know

I'm supposed to get curious. I'm trying. So what did I miss in the survey process?"

"Julia's right, but it's not just your fault," said Redley. "Any of us could have reminded you or chimed in ourselves. Shared responsibility, right?"

"We had planned to tell them they could vote in town hall and at the library if they didn't have a computer," reminded Fletcher. "I could have told them that. I was the last one presenting."

"Also, now that I think of it," added Mark, "we definitely should have emphasized what we're going to do with the vote or what we're not going to do with it, I guess. Mayor, you mentioned it at the beginning, but in the next meetings, I think we need to remind them again at the end that this isn't a binding vote. Make sure they have clear expectations."

They all agreed that that was particularly important and decided that each of them should mention it at the end of their sections. They had a few more ideas and then they wrapped up.

"Thanks, Julia," said Redley, uncurling her legs from under her. "I'm glad we did this right away. I keep meaning to remember this for my own meetings. Take a few minutes after they're over to review what happened, before rushing off."

Cesar stood up. "Good work, all. Really good work. Not just now, or tonight's meeting. But everything that led up to tonight. I knew I had picked the right people. Now go home and get a good night's sleep," said Cesar, frowning in playful sternness. "We've got to do this again at lunchtime tomorrow."

They all groaned as they pushed themselves out of their chairs.

"Before you go," added Cesar, "I just want to tell you all how much I appreciate your commitment to this project. I know it's taken way more time than you expected. More time than I told you it would take. It means a lot to me, and it means a lot to the town." He shook hands with the men and gave Redley a hug.

Redley grinned and punched his arm playfully. "Aw, shucks, Chief. You'll make us blush."

Mark smiled. "I don't know about that, but it is nice to be appreciated."

"Thank you, Mayor," said Fletcher thoughtfully. "Thank you for saying that. It matters. Your work was good, too, by the way. And appreciated."

Mark, Redley, and Fletcher walked out together. Julia stayed for a minute on the stage with Cesar.

Pause and Reflect

Chapter 38

"That was good, what you said to them," Julia told Cesar.

"I meant it."

"I know you did. That's why it had an impact on them. You noticed that, didn't you?"

"I guess so," said Cesar. "Yes, I did, actually. It means a lot to me, like I said. They've come a long way. We've come a long way together. Especially thanks to you. Now that I think of it, did you notice Fletcher? He really seemed pleased there at the end, didn't he?"

"You know he's working hard on keeping his assistant. I think it probably struck him how easily you offered your thanks from the heart. He got to notice how it felt to receive it. Maybe you've given him something to think about."

"Speaking of learning, I think I need to go find Mel Schroom, don't I?" Cesar said as he helped Julia into her coat.

"I think you do," she said.

They walked up the aisle of the auditorium and into the crisp night air. The moon was just a sliver and the sky was full of stars. As they said goodbye, Julia had just one suggestion for Cesar.

"When you meet Mel, just remember to pay attention to both the strategic and the relational," she reminded him. "Connection before action."

"Oh, I won't forget that. Don't worry," said Cesar, grinning.

He drove home thinking about the meeting, Schroom, and Julia's words, but he liked rephrasing them as strategic and intimate. It made him smile.

He was still smiling when he joined his wife in the kitchen. She was fixing them each a cocktail.

"I watched the meeting on the cable channel," she said. "You all did a very good job, I thought."

"Thanks, Kelly," he said as he took the drink she offered him and leaned over to kiss her. "But I don't think you're entirely objective."

"Hey, wait. I always tell you the truth. Some of your speeches are better than others. I thought all of you were very engaging tonight, a good combination of the vision and the facts."

"Yes, we were strategic and intimate," Cesar said, grinning wickedly when Kelly looked startled. He explained what Julia had taught them about the importance of combining both.

"Did you hear the guy at the end?" he asked.

"Yes, who was that? I didn't recognize him."

"That was Mel Schroom."

She looked up at him in surprise. "Really! Wow. He looks so different with his hair cut and those glasses."

"I thought so too. I didn't recognize him either."

"He's like a different person without those dreadlocks. He even wore a tie tonight!"

"He used to look like the campus radical. Now he almost looks like an accountant," agreed Cesar.

"Well, it was over two years ago. I wonder where he's been since then?"

"I don't know. I guess I can ask him when I talk to him."

"You've got a meeting set up?"

"No, but obviously he's back in town. I'll see if I can get together with him tomorrow," said Cesar. "Let's stop talking about him. It's a beautiful night. Put on your coat and let's take our cocktails outside. I'll light a fire in the fire pit."

Chapter 39

The next morning Cesar asked his aide to find Schroom. "Get me an appointment. Cancel anything in my schedule, if you have to," he said.

Then he looked up Schroom's morning blog on his computer. The further he read, the angrier he got. He picked up the phone and called Fletcher.

"You know what that guy has done now?" Cesar said, as soon as Fletcher answered. "He's encouraging people to vote for a casino on the survey. He's telling them to lobby us to make sure the online version allows for a write-in vote."

"That's ridiculous," said Fletcher. "He can't do that."

"He did. Look, I'll send you a link to his blog. I'll send it to Mark and Redley, too."

"We have to stop him. He's got to be making this whole casino thing up!" Fletcher's voice was getting louder. "This is outrageous! It's not ethical."

"Read the blog. I'll see if I can get Mark and Redley on the phone and then call you back."

"This is bullshit!" said Redley, as soon as they were all on the line. "He can't do this. We've got the survey all set up. It's ready to go."

"It's not logical," said Mark. "No one knows if the casino has even a kernel of truth to it."

"People of his kind aren't logical," said Fletcher. "Extremists don't listen to logic. We have to destroy his credibility."

"So let me ask a question. Is anyone reading his stuff?" asked Mark. "Does this matter as much to anyone else as it does to us?"

"Actually, it does. It's not so much that our townspeople are reading his blog," said Cesar. "What my aides tell me is that our local reporters are. In fact, I've already heard a local radio reporter quoting him. It's also on the website of the Coastal Daily. And the regional papers are picking it up."

"Crap!" said Redley. "What do we do? Can we make him look bad?"

"I don't think that's the right approach," said Cesar. "Julia's encouraged me to meet with him and I've got my staff working on an appointment right now. Even if we could discredit him somehow…. Which I agree sounds appealing at times…. But even if we could do it…"

"What?" asked Fletcher. "You have an objection?"

"I don't know. It doesn't meet my sniff test. It doesn't feel right," said Cesar.

"I can't believe you're saying this," said Fletcher. "You of all people. Remember the past?"

"We shouldn't lower ourselves to his level," said Mark.

They were all silent for a long time.

"Look. Let me see what he says when I meet with him," said Cesar. "Redley, if we need to include a write-in space for ideas would that be possible at this late date?"

"Sure. Because it's online it's easy to change," she answered quickly. "It will just take a bit longer to tally, that's all. I suppose we could actually put a casino as one of the drop down choices that people could vote for if you want."

"No," said Fletcher. "That makes no sense."

"I hear you, Fletcher," said Cesar. "Still, if the change is easy, maybe we should wait until we finish all our community meetings. We've only had one. Let's gauge public opinion before we do anything. And I'll meet with him. What do you all say to that?"

"I'm wondering what we would do if the majority voted for a casino?" asked Redley.

"That would be awful," moaned Mark. "No. I can't believe that could happen. Not in this town. People wouldn't want that. Not our neighbors."

"There wouldn't be much we could do with a vote like that," said Cesar, "much as you know I'd hate it. We're going for the grant and a casino isn't a choice we could get funded. Unfortunately, the grant does stipulate that no other viable commercial option can be available. Right now no developer has come forward, so we're okay." There was a knock at his door and when he swiveled around he saw his aide in the doorway. "Hold on everyone. I need a minute." He clicked on the mute button.

"Mel Schroom will be here at three p.m.," his aide said. The mayor nodded and clicked the sound on his phone. They were still talking about the possibility of a casino.

"Listen, folks, I'm going to meet with Schroom later. See what I can find out. Maybe mend some fences. If there's anything you should know, I'll get back to you. Meanwhile, we'll stay steady. Besides, it's not likely the town would go for it."

Pause and Reflect

Chapter 40

When Redley hung up, she went back to reviewing the spread sheet on her computer screen. She had tracked every interruption for days. As she looked it over she started to notice a pattern. People turned to her from every department. She had categorized the questions.

Some were about her opinion. Most of those were from folks in the marketing department and the retail shop. Some were technical procedures and problems. Most of those were from the brewing floor and a couple from the meadery on the new experimental meads they were trying for the season. There were also payroll questions and vendor questions from the finance department. Then there were a bunch of interruptions from the sales team which were mostly about negotiations with distributors and some of the interstate shipping requirements.

She was tempted to immediately create a column of solutions. Instead she just sat and contemplated the screen in front of her.

There was a knock on her door.

"Redley? Do you have a minute?" Joe, her sales manager, was in the doorway with a sheaf of papers in his hand. "I want to go over this new client proposal."

Redley waved him in. "Come sit a minute," she said, and moved around her desk to one of the wing chairs. Joe came toward the desk but didn't move to sit down.

"This will be quick," he said. "I don't want to take much time but I need your input." He handed her one of the papers from his stack. "Take a look."

She took the paper and looked at it quickly then looked up.

"What do you need from me?" she asked.

He shrugged. "Is the bulk discount acceptable? You always like to go over everything before it goes out. That's what you always say."

"Do I always say that? I guess I do. What do you think about this discount?"

"This is a good customer. Bigger order than usual," explained Joe.

"Is this the right discount for the size order?" Redley asked.

"I think we need to take care of them. It's fair and it's worth it to keep their business."

"Should we do anything else?" asked Redley.

He stopped and thought. Then he offered up several new ideas to give better service and delivery. "Actually, if we did those, we could offer a smaller discount and they'd still be thrilled, I'd bet. It would cost us less, too."

"Great suggestions. I wouldn't have thought of those. Go for it." Redley handed the paper back to him. "You can make these decisions in the future, can't you?"

"Sure," said Joe. "But don't you want to go over them? It's your company."

"I trust you. Plus, I should start to move my focus more to big picture strategy than all the details of each and every contract."

"Maybe," said Joe hesitantly, looking a bit confused.

"I think I should," said Redley, frowning. "I've been micromanaging you, haven't I?"

"Uh… Well… you don't treat me any different from anyone else. You've got your finger in everything here. Figure you like it that way."

"Okay, maybe I do. Maybe I did," Redley corrected herself. "But maybe I shouldn't be, that's what I'm trying to say. Maybe I should be letting you and others do your jobs and solve the problems without me getting involved."

"Well, you have kept the training wheels on longer than any other boss I've ever had."

"Why didn't you tell me?" asked Redley, getting up and fiddling with her letter opener. "I just want things to go right."

"Redley, it's not for me to tell you how to run your business. It bugged me a lot at first, you hanging over everything. I never had a female boss before so I thought…"

"What?" interrupted Redley.

Joe put up both hands defensively. "Let me finish! As I got to know you better I saw it was just how much you cared. I'm used to it by now. Plus, it seemed to work. Even though our growth has leveled off recently, I've still got distributors calling me. I like success as much as the next guy."

Redley leaned against her desk and shook her head.

"How about if we do things differently from now on," said Redley. "I'm thinking you could take over the proposal review for all the regular deals but keep me in the loop on anything unusual. What do you think?"

"Aren't you going to feel in the dark?"

"Probably. I'll just have to get used to it, won't I?" said Redley, setting the letter opener down. "Tell me if I start getting too close, okay? Or solving your problems for you. Just remind me to ask questions rather than tell you what to do."

"Well, okay. I guess I can do that," said Joe.

"Just to get started, let's review the last quarter of new contracts together. See which ones I should have been involved in and which ones you could have handled alone. That way, we'll be clear we're on the same page."

"Makes sense. Starting out that way might be better, because, frankly, I don't want to feel you're going to be second guessing my judgment."

They made an appointment to sit down to do a review the next morning. When he walked out of the room, Redley picked up the phone and called Julia.

"Look, do you have a minute?" she asked when Julia answered. "I wanted to share some progress with you."

"I have about five minutes before my coaching call."

"I'll only take two." She explained to Julia what had just transpired with her sales manager. "I took a step but now I need some help paying attention to where I can be spending my time differently," she concluded.

"Things that only you, as the leader, can do?" asked Julia.

"Definitely. He basically told me I've been holding on too tight. Anyway, we set up a new process for him to take care of things on his own unless he really needs me."

"How does it feel?"

"Good. A little scary—like I'll be left out of the loop when I need to be in it. But I guess I have to live with it."

"That's a choice," reminded Julia.

"You're right. I am choosing this new path."

"If it doesn't work, you can course correct, right?"

"Right," said Redley with relief. "That feels a little less final."

"Being a leader is all about course correction," said Julia. "I read somewhere that a plane traveling from one coast to the other is off course more than it's on, but gets there through constant course corrections."

"I like that. Look, I know you have to go. But I'm going to need more help. Can we talk about working together? I can see I need help to see what I don't see, if that makes any sense. I'm too alone in this role. I need your questions. They help me think."

"Call me when you're ready," said Julia.

"Will I see you at the public meeting today?" asked Redley. "I wonder if that Mel Schroom will be there."

Chapter 41

The lunchtime public meeting at the Northside Library went well. The audience was a mixture of retirees, a few mothers with their toddlers in tow, plus a smattering of working folks who brought lunch with them.

Julia wasn't there and Mel Schroom wasn't in attendance. No one mentioned the casino. Before the meeting, the mayor asked the rest of them whether they should bring it up themselves and ask what people thought. They decided to mention the rumor and if people seemed interested they'd ask for pubic opinion on it, but when it came up no one in the audience followed up with a question or comment. The committee took that as a good sign.

On his way back to the office, Cesar picked up some lunch and brought it back to his desk. As he was eating he reminded himself about Julia's advice. Connection before action. Balancing intimate and strategic. Getting curious.

When Mel Schroom arrived, wearing a white shirt, red tie and navy blazer over blue jeans, Cesar was ready.

After shaking hands, Cesar ushered Mel toward the two guest chairs in front of the desk and sat down opposite him.

"So Mr. Schroom," Cesar said.

"Yes, Mr. Mayor."

"Please, call me Cesar. I know you've got questions for me, and I've got a couple for you, but first I thought it might make sense to take a few minutes to get to know each other. Is that okay with you?"

"I'm not sure why you'd want to waste the time, Mr. Mayor," said Schroom. He crossed and re-crossed his legs. "I'd just like to know more about your committee."

"It won't be a waste," said Cesar, patiently. "So you're back living in town?"

Schroom nodded.

"You buy a house or did you move in with your folks. They're on Elm Street, right?"

"Yes, but that's not…"

"Are you…. married?" asked Cesar.

"I don't think this is relevant," said Schroom quickly.

"Girlfriend?" Cesar smiled.

Schroom frowned and then gave a slight shake of his head. "I'd like to understand your committee…"

"Kids?" said Cesar, then gave a brief laugh and shrugged. "No, I guess not."

"No." said Schroom.

"Ahh," said Cesar, awkwardly. "So you're a news blogger now?"

"You already know that, Mr. Mayor, so I'm not sure why you're asking."

"Do you do something else as well?" continued Cesar, sounding falsely cheerful.

"I do, but I'd really like to…"

"Oh, yes? And what's that?"

"Why does this matter?" asked Schroom. "I'm the reporter. Why are you interviewing me? My private life isn't why you called me here. Now let's get on to the reasons for your choice of the Blue Ribbon Committee, as you call it."

"I guess I was just curious," said Cesar after a pause, his fingers tapping on the arm of his chair.

Schroom just sat there, staring at Cesar. Then he answered. "Making a living in this town isn't easy. I write, I bartend. And so I don't have to do it forever, grad school at night. Now are we done with twenty questions?"

"Huh! Good for you. What in?"

Again Schroom sat there for a long time, as if weighing whether or not he'd answer. Finally he did.

"Law."

Cesar sat back in his chair. "That's interesting," he said slowly. It was his turn to pause and consider. "I'm wondering, does your interest in our town project have anything to do with your law studies?"

"Does that matter?" asked Schroom, almost in a challenging tone.

"I suppose not," said Cesar carefully. "I was just wondering if you had any interest in going into government."

"No!"

"That was definite! Don't act like it's something dirty," said Cesar, his annoyance clear.

Schroom raised his eyebrows.

Cesar took a breath and kept pushing forward. "If that's not what you want to do, what's your interest in law? Real estate?

"No! Please! Public defense."

"That's a worthy goal," said Cesar, after a moment, obviously working to hold on to his patience.

Schroom's eyes narrowed. "That's enough of the personal stuff! I don't need or appreciate your assessment of my goals, positive or negative. They're personal."

"Hey, there," said Cesar, losing his battle to stay curious. "You got personal with me in my last campaign. So guess what? I don't appreciate your assessment of my committee choices in your blog."

"That's not personal. Or was it?" Schroom added quickly.

"I resent that. You implied in your blog that I might have chosen my committee because of political reasons, campaign reasons." Cesar's face was getting red.

"You had some other reason?" Schroom asked quickly.

"Of course. Good reasons," said Cesar, jumping up out of his chair. "Important strategic reasons, damn it!"

"Ahhh. You have some pretty well-heeled members on that committee."

"That's ridiculous! They are successful leaders in town! That's why they were picked." Cesar's voice got louder.

Schroom sat silently. Cesar saw the slight smile flicker across Schroom's face.

"Their success," echoed Schroom. "Financial success."

Cesar stopped pacing and sat down carefully behind his desk, grabbing a pile of papers and neatening them by tapping the pile over and over on the desk. He looked at his wife's picture. Her mother was in the background of the photo, looking a lot like Julia. That made him pause. He took a deep breath and got up and came back to sit opposite Schroom in the guest chair.

"Do you have something against me personally? Did I do something to you that I'm not aware of to give you such a bad opinion of me?" Cesar asked.

"You're a politician."

"What's wrong with that?"

"You represent big government and the establishment," said Schroom. "Plus you never return my calls. You never respond to my emails."

"Oh, please! That is so sixties. What century is this? This is town government, not a political machine. And I certainly don't represent the establishment."

"Of course you do. And I wasn't born in the sixties. Look at this office. Your great big mahogany desk. The American flag to the left, the state flag to the right. This is the establishment, my friend."

"I don't think we're friends," shot back Cesar. "Besides, what's wrong with flags?" He started to stand up again but then settled back into his chair, taking a deep breath. "Wait a minute. Let's get back to the point. To the grant process and the Blue Ribbon Committee." Cesar paused awkwardly then began speaking more slowly. "I picked the three I did because I wanted diversity of background, diversity of gender, and diversity of perspective. In case you're interested, they're so different, they don't agree on anything. That's why we're having these public meetings. We're wanting public opinion to help us reach consensus."

"Really?" asked Schroom blandly. "Diversity? I don't see anyone who's black."

"No, but we have me, right? I'm Hispanic. Besides, that's not the only diversity that matters."

"Really? You say they don't agree? According to my research, the grant requires a unanimous decision. So does that mean you aren't going to be able to apply?"

"No! That is not what it means. This committee will apply and the town will ultimately benefit from this generous grant. You can put that in your blog. I think we're done here."

"Okay, Mr. Mayor. If that's what you want." Schroom pushed back his chair and almost bolted from the room.

"Wait, wait. What about the casino?" asked Cesar, remembering the questions he wanted to ask. "Who's your source? What can you tell me?"

Schroom shook his head as he went through the door.

Cesar followed him toward the door, then he, too, shook his head and walked back to his desk, sinking into his chair and swiveling to look out the window.

"That went well," he said aloud to his reflection in the glass. "Damn it! I didn't even get any information from him! The whole idea of connection didn't work at all." Suddenly he swiveled back around to his desk and slammed his fist down. "What's that blog headline going to be next?"

Cesar didn't have long to wait.

Pause and Reflect

Chapter 42

"Mayor says Blue Ribbon Committee Can't Make Decisions," Cesar read on his computer, just thirty minutes after Schroom had exited his office.

"Goddammit!" said Cesar scrolling down the screen. His aide came to his door.

"You need me?"

"No. Listen to this crap." The mayor tilted the screen on his computer slightly and read aloud. 'Mayor's high paid committee is in total disagreement, despite their well-paid consultant. They can't do their job because they can't get along so they're asking the town to do it.'" Cesar looked up and frowned. "Get Julia on the line for me."

"I didn't do so good," said Cesar when he was finally connected to Julia an hour later.

"What do you mean?" she asked.

"The meeting with that blogger reporter or whatever he is. Schroom."

"Ahhh."

"Yeah. Ahhh. Say aah like going to the dentist. I feel as if I got my teeth drilled without Novocain. I just don't like that kid. I tried, I really tried."

"So what did you try?" asked Julia.

"I tried connecting. Intimate, right? Connection before action, you said. But he wouldn't connect back."

"Did he give you any indication why?"

"No. He came in with a chip on his shoulder."

"He was resistant. Didn't trust you," said Julia.

"You got it. That's for sure. No way he trusted me. Nor I him, for that matter. No way."

"Okay. Any idea why?"

"I'm establishment, he said. Do you believe that?"

"That sounds like the sixties," said Julia.

Cesar laughed for the first time in hours. "Yeah, that's what I said. I don't think he liked it."

"What else? Any other reason he gave for being resistant? You say he didn't connect?"

"Right away. I tried. I really tried. I asked him lots of personal questions. Tried to connect. He wasn't having it."

"Personal questions?"

"Yes. Like you said. I asked him the questions, you know, like about his marital status. Whether he'd bought a house."

"Hmmmm."

"What does that mean?" asked Cesar with a defensive tone.

"Are you interested in feedback?"

"Come on, Julia. Don't fool around with me now. I'm not in the mood."

"I get that," she assured him. "That's why I wondered if you really wanted feedback now. Are you ready to take anything in yet?"

Cesar was silent for a minute. "No, I guess. I see your point. I'm still angry. I don't want to hear I did anything wrong."

"Wow. That's great awareness."

"So what is it I did wrong?" asked Cesar after a long pause.

Julia laughed. "Okay, but I'm not sure it was wrong, so to speak. I wasn't there. I can only judge by the outcome. You were trying to connect and you didn't, right?"

"Right. For sure."

"Connection isn't always about personal questions," said Julia. "That could work with someone you know well. With some people they could feel like it's invasion of privacy. It depends on the individual. Connection is about finding common ground. Getting curious about the person in front of you."

"I did. I asked questions."

"Apparently not questions he wanted to answer. Let's stop for a moment. Put yourself in his shoes. He's been calling and calling you. All of a sudden he gets his audience with you. What would you have felt in his place?"

Cesar just sat there. "I don't know. Probably annoyed."

"Why?"

"Well, I'd feel like I'd been ignored. Then asked a bunch of personal questions. But Julia, that's what you told me to do," said Cesar.

"Hold on. As you say, you didn't return his many attempts to contact you. You ignored him, in your own words. Suddenly you ask him to come in and ask him all kinds of personal questions."

"Okay, so in his shoes... You're right," agreed Cesar.

"It's not right or wrong that matters. It's what works and what doesn't. That's where the relational part comes in. It's not about questions. It's about staying aware of where the other person is and what they might need. So think about it. What might he have needed?"

"Oh geez. I guess I could have started with an apology for not returning his calls. I never even thought of that," said Cesar ruefully.

"Then what?" asked Julia.

"Let's see. I could have asked some questions about the place he works for, I guess. Or what brought him back to town. I don't know. They might have annoyed him, too."

"They might have, or maybe not. We won't know. Did he get annoyed right away?"

"Well, he didn't even want to answer my first question," said Cesar, spinning a pencil on his desk as he recalled the conversation.

"And what did you do?"

"Yeah. I get it. I ignored the fact he didn't want to answer and kept on pushing him. All I found out was that he wants to be a public defender."

"That's impressive," remarked Julia.

"That's what I said. He didn't like that."

"What, that you said it?"

"That I had an opinion one way or another, I guess," said Cesar.

"Judgment is judgment. If you can judge positively, you can judge negatively."

"Yeah. He said he didn't appreciate my opinion. That's when I sort of blew."

"Ahhh. You blew?" repeated Julia neutrally.

"I told him I didn't appreciate his opinions about me in his blog. Then we sort of went at it and he stormed out."

"Okay."

"What do you mean, okay?"

"Well, what's done is done. You made a choice. So how can I help you now?"

"What do you mean?" asked Cesar.

"You called me. What is it you'd like help with?"

"I'm not sure. I guess I need to think about what to do next. I don't know. Help me. What do you think?"

"I think the hardest type of resistance to break down is when there's not trust. You said it yourself. You don't trust him, and he doesn't trust you."

"So what can I do about it?"

"I'm still curious whether you see any clues that could help you now. Did you go to him or did he come to you?"

"He came to me," said Cesar.

"Was there anything in what he said? Any specific complaint about you at all? Anything you'd done? Any reference to anything that seemed to concern him?"

"Well, he didn't like the personal questions. And... he did say I hadn't returned his phone calls or emails."

"So what do you think your choices are?" asked Julia.

"I could go see him again. I could email him an apology. I could.... What? I can't really think of anything else. Other than I need to do my own research on this damn casino thing. He's not going to tell me anything."

"Should he?"

"I guess not," said Cesar grudgingly. "I recognize that they protect their sources or they won't get any more information from anyone. Look, I've got another meeting so I need to wrap up. Thanks for calming me down and making me pay attention."

"You may not want to hear this just yet, but remember that whatever happened in that room was because of what you both brought into it. Not just him and not just you. Maybe think about what you'd want you to do if you stood in his shoes right now."

Cesar hung up and collected his files for the next meeting. As he left his office, he asked his aide to call in all favors and see what they could find out about the casino rumor.

Pause and Reflect

Chapter 43

The morning was warmer and Fletcher walked into the bank without his overcoat. He greeted the front receptionist and took the elevator up. Although it was still early, his leadership team were already in their offices. He made a point of stopping in to speak to each of them.

He turned the lights on in his office and got files out of his briefcase. When he opened his computer, he found a message from the mayor. "Call me as soon as you can."

He picked up the phone and dialed.

"Thanks for getting back so quickly," said Cesar. "We need to find out more about this casino rumor. I'm having my aides check on it, but I wondered if you could get some of your commercial lenders looking into it."

Fletcher shook his head. "You know a big casino developer wouldn't be coming to a bank my size," he warned.

"I know you said that but I just thought maybe some of your guys might have heard something on the street."

"I'll see what I can do, Mayor," said Fletcher. "No promises," he added, standing up when he noticed his assistant arriving.

"Morning, Angie," he called out as he hung up. Her greeting was muffled as she turned away to hang up her coat. He got up and walked out to her desk.

"I didn't even wear a coat this morning. It feels a bit like spring coming, doesn't it?"

She smiled. "It's a tease. You and I both know the wind will turn and blow cold off the water."

"How's your daughter's science project coming?"

"She presents today," said Angie.

"Do you want to be there?"

Angie shook her head. "I asked her if I could attend but she told me in no uncertain terms she didn't want me there."

Fletcher nodded. "I've heard that myself. Listen, once you get settled, can you see if you can find Steve and Janet? They're probably out on the road somewhere but the Mayor wants me to see if they know anything about that casino rumor."

"Oh, yeah. I read that blog yesterday afternoon."

"I didn't see it," said Fletcher.

"I'll get right on it," she said, as she put her purse in the desk drawer and opened her computer. "When you get a chance, go look at it. It's pretty tough on you all."

Chapter 44

T he remainder of the community information meetings were held without disruption, except one, where Mel Schroom attended again and spoke to the advantages of immediate jobs with a casino.

The mayor's staff had been collecting a lot of reference data on potential tax implications, traffic, economic value and true job creation on casinos that the committee members were able to provide at the meeting. Neither the mayor nor Fletcher's lenders had found any evidence that a casino developer was interested in the grant site, but they did uncover some unusual and significant interest in large open parcels throughout the area.

Redley had first amended the online survey to include a casino choice at the mayor's request. Then, with no substantiating evidence, he had her remove it, not wanting to mislead the town that it was a realistic choice. At the last minute, he asked her to put in a place for a write-in vote where people could opt for the casino or anything else they had in mind, but it was topped with a disclaimer that write-in votes could not be part of the grant and were only to allow them to express other opinions.

The survey went out immediately after the last of the community meetings, and two days later the final results were tabulated and the Blue Ribbon Committee met back in the town hall conference room.

"Here's what we've got," said Cesar. "I'm not sure what you're going to think of this or what we should do, but I have to say that I have confidence in us as a team that we'll come up with a great final proposal for the grant."

Julia looked across just as Cesar looked at her. She smiled and nodded.

He passed the tabulations around the table. "On the first page, the votes are broken down by precinct. The second page has the summary."

They all flipped over.

"Awwww, man," said Redley, scanning through the numbers quickly. "This is really disappointing, and tough to know what to do with. So many people said the economy is what matters in this town. That was mentioned over and over at every gathering. With all due respect for the other proposals, I was the only one with a real economic solution. Then it comes out lowest with only twenty-four percent. That little customer survey Fletcher did months ago was far more even. I don't get it."

"That was more weighted by our commercial clients, Redley," explained Fletcher. "The town survey is a broader demographic."

"It's not likely they'd see it that way," said Mark softly. "People look out for what's good for them personally. Probably they couldn't see themselves ever going into a business incubator. They don't have a frame of reference. Maybe they see the businesses and jobs being hatched as coming from outside of town and going back out of town. They didn't see it as a benefit to them. I heard a bit of that thinking from patients."

Redley nodded. "I should have included the stipulation that any businesses growing out of the incubator would have to stay in town for at least five years. We talked about that at the meetings but it wasn't in the survey. This is a business decision with business implications but we don't have a town full of business people. Look at these results. The casino as a write-in got a decent number of votes. They voted for what they'd use themselves."

"The casino only got nine percent," said Fletcher, circling the number with his pencil. "Although that may be a statistically significant number for a write-in. Mayor, do you know?" Cesar shook his head. Fletcher flipped the page back to look at the precincts. "Most of the casino votes seem to be concentrated from one precinct. The other precincts are pretty even."

"That's Schroom's precinct," said Cesar. "Those were the meetings he attended."

"Precinct Four—aren't they furthest from the mill building?" asked Fletcher.

"That's true," said Cesar. "So maybe they didn't worry about negative impact on them personally."

"I guess more people see value for themselves in your proposal, Mark," noticed Fletcher. "You clearly carried this vote with thirty-six percent."

"A lot of people supported your cultural center, though," said Mark. "It's not a done deal. Don't you think this is almost a tie?"

"Which brings us back to where we began," said Cesar. "We've gone out to the people. Even included the possibility of a casino. We've got their feedback. We told them it wasn't binding. Now what shall we do with it? We need to publish it with our response. I just got these results and they still aren't validated so I can hold off today. But the Freedom of Information Act folks will be breathing down my throat if I don't get it out promptly."

"Especially Schroom," said Fletcher.

"Especially Schroom," agreed Cesar.

"We did get some pretty good feedback from people about asking for their input," commented Redley. "It was still worth doing, don't you think?" She looked around the table curiously. "Doc? This was your idea, what do you think?"

"Definitely. People liked that we asked them. They really liked those community meetings," said Mark.

"In a way, I'm not surprised," said Fletcher. "We got more input but it doesn't take us to a decision. The data doesn't point to any one overwhelming preference. We, as leaders, still need to make the choice. Do you agree, Redley?"

"You're really right, Fletch," said Redley, tapping her pencil on her teeth. "The good thing is that they are all interesting to the town. Any one of the proposals could work. We'll never know once we choose whether another would have been better. We have no crystal ball."

"So what do you propose we do?" asked Cesar. "We've only got one month left and that includes having to write the whole proposal. Anyone think we should get a neutral third party to come in here and evaluate all three on the business merits?"

"That's crazy," said Fletcher. "We don't have time for that. Plus we've already looked at the upsides and downsides of each proposal ourselves."

"I don't know," said Redley. "The grant-makers may not accept what we've done. After all, they may not consider projections from your bank since you're involved with the committee."

"No, don't worry about that. They'll validate all the financials in the grant proposals themselves," said Cesar.

"I'm wondering..." said Mark, leaning forward. "No, I guess..." he added, then leaned back in his chair.

"What?" asked Cesar. "You sound like you've got an idea."

"Maybe we should ask for Julia's thoughts first," said Mark, turning in his chair to where Julia sat quietly in front of the window.

"Right," said Cesar. "You've been quiet. What do you suggest?" he asked.

Julia shook her head. "You've got to decide how to make this decision. Look back at your problem. What's the problem you're trying to solve in town?"

"It's an economic problem," said Redley, repeating her earlier thought. "That's what's been so frustrating. We have an economic problem that needs an economic solution. We want a vibrant and lively town and we need growth for that."

"It's a community issue," said Mark. "The economic problem has just been a symptom of a community exodus. People that grew up here have gotten old and moved south. They're in the snow belt. We need to be attractive to young people again with a community center so the town will be active and interactive."

"It is about attraction, but we need to have a central magnet, a regional attraction that puts this town back on the map, especially with the wealthier demographic," said

Fletcher. "We want a thriving town full of people and shops and activity and culture."

"Who's right?" asked Julia looking from one to another with a smile.

"We sound like we did at the first meeting, don't we, Julia?" asked Mark.

"Wait," Cesar looked around the table and back down at the voting tabulations. "You're all right," he said. "Look at this. The town agrees. You're all right. In a way, you all agree. You're using different words to say the same thing. Vibrant, thriving, active, interactive."

"Is it possible..." said Redley tentatively, "that we could do some part of all three?"

"That's what I was thinking before," said Mark.

"I don't know," said Fletcher, with a warning tone in his voice. "Could increase our costs significantly with that many uses."

"We wouldn't have to do everything right away. But think of the synergy," said Redley, clearly excited with the idea.

"I like it," said Mark. "I like it a lot. What costs are you concerned about, Fletch?"

"Operational costs, mostly. The construction costs probably will shift some, but ultimately if we build out all the space we've got the same square footage of construction. Actually, Redley's proposal has the cheapest construction costs because it's just office space. But for operating, we'd need three staffs."

"Will we?" challenged Redley. "I'm not sure. I've seen a cooperative venture like this in Canada when I went up for the brewer's conference last year. Or something like this. In their case they had a hockey school, a retail and restaurant complex, and a local history museum all operating together. They had a single operational staff for the businesses but a divisional head of each area supervising programs and marketing."

"It is true that several of our larger commercial loan customers have different business divisions under one leadership team," said Fletcher, starting to look energized.

"Hey, we said we wanted to create jobs anyway," said Mark. "Maybe we can have more part-time or internship opportunities or even volunteers involved with this arrangement."

"Chief," said Redley, "I know we had the architect and engineering consultants available to us early on. Can we re-engage them for a quick review of what the space there could actually accommodate before we go any further?"

"Wait a minute," said Fletcher. "Just wait a minute! Let's stick with operational costs before you go charging off to redesign the space."

"Right," said Redley, a flush flooding from her neck up through her cheeks. She looked over at Julia and took a deep breath to slow herself down, and then turned back to Fletcher. "What would we need to do to address the question of higher operational costs in a way that would satisfy you?"

"It's not just about satisfying me, Redley," said Fletcher slowly. "It's about meeting the criteria of the grant. It's about sustainability of the project once it's built. You know that."

"Yes, Fletcher, I know all that," said Redley slowly, as if trying to keep her patience. "I just figure we can solve it. I can see I'm going too fast for you. I'm trying to slow down."

"You don't need to slow down for me," said Fletcher. "I've been around this block a lot longer than you…"

"Oh, don't pull that age and experience thing again at this point," said Redley, leaning into the table, her voice rising.

"I'm not pulling anything," said Fletcher loudly, leaning in toward Redley. "The fact of the matter is…."

All of a sudden, they both stopped and looked at each other and shook their heads.

"Old habits…" said Redley.

"Die hard," finished Fletcher.

"Look, you two," interrupted Cesar. "You sound like an old married couple. We've come too far for you all to start back fighting."

They laughed. "We're fine," they both said in unison. "We're over it," added Redley and winked at Fletcher. He nodded back at her with a hint mischief in his smile.

"Right," said Redley. "So Fletcher, you're our numbers person, okay? What if you and your staff evaluate the numbers using what we already have, but making some educated assumptions on a combined management structure." Fletcher nodded. "I'm willing to bring the ideas to the consultants for a space review."

"Wait. I think we should identify what we think is crucial in each plan," said Mark. "Then, could we come back with answers by Thursday afternoon? Fletch, Red? You have the real work to do."

"I'll make sure I can," said Redley.

Fletcher nodded. " I agree. I don't see that we have a choice with that deadline looming."

"All right, then it's decided," said Redley.

Cesar saluted. "Yes, sir, Chief."

Redley laughed. "But right now let's…"

"Make a list of the priorities from each plan," finished Mark.

"I could entertain that," agreed Fletcher. Cesar nodded.

They got to work and went through four pages of flip chart paper, adding and taking away elements of each plan until they had a list they could all agree on, including a common area to be used by all three. Cesar added in a few comments here and there but mostly just sat and watched with a bemused expression on his face as they raced along together. When they were done, he took a few minutes to have them summarize the decisions they'd made. "I'll get to the press this afternoon with the survey votes. You seem like you think we could be ready to go back out to the public with a plan ASAP."

"For public disclosure and to get that grant written once we make the decision," agreed Redley. "That's no small task."

Everyone agreed. Cesar reviewed the grant components and explained which pieces he was having his staff assemble, such as the demographics and economic data the committee had already reviewed.

Julia and Cesar stayed at the table after the committee members had left.

"For the first time, I'm really excited," said Cesar. "I think this could work. Would be terrific for the town." He looked out the window. "Maybe it would be my legacy," he added.

Julia stood up and put on her jacket. "A fine legacy it would be," she said.

"You know, I hardly had to do anything this meeting. They all were practically working without me."

"That's what happens with a high performing team. The leader just gives support, and then stays out of the way."

"I like this a whole lot better than when I felt like the referee in a prize fight."

"Sure. When you're in that prize fight stage, it's hard work," said Julia. "You've got to keep them in the ring to work things out, make sure they fight fair. Try to help them build trust with one another. That's what got them to this compromise they couldn't even see before. The leader does different work at different stages," agreed Julia. "Now you just get out of their way."

"I feel like I'm forgetting something, though."

"How are you doing with Schroom?" asked Julia.

"Right! I wanted to tell you I've decided to go to him this time. One last try at mending fences, I guess."

"Good luck," said Julia.

"I don't know if I need luck, so much as I need to pay more attention to him and less to myself," said Cesar. "No time like the present."

Chapter 45

Cesar picked up the phone and was able to reach Mel Schroom directly.

"I'm sorry about our last meeting," said Cesar. "I wonder if we could try again?"

Mel didn't say anything.

"I'd like to come down to your office, if that's okay. I have the votes to share with you."

Mel said he'd be in all afternoon.

Cesar walked out into the sunshine, a copy of the vote results in his hand. It was such a nice day, he left his car and walked down the hill to the Valley Net News office. He'd never been in the doors before but he'd driven by many times.

A girl in a sweatshirt and jeans looked up from her computer when he walked in. She took an earpiece out of her ear, untangling the white wire from her long hair.

"Can I help you?" she asked Cesar.

"Mel Schroom, please. He said he'd be in?"

"He's due back any minute," she said after picking up her cell phone to check the time. "You can wait, if you want." She pointed to a single plastic chair by a stack of newspapers and magazines piled on the floor in the corner.

He sat down and picked up the top magazine. It was a dog eared magazine about computer gaming. He put it down and searched through the pile. Before he found something he was interested in reading, Mel Schroom walked in.

"Mayor," he said. "I didn't expect you so quickly."

"Please call me Cesar." He held up the papers in his hand. "I have the votes and I figure you'd like to see them right away. No one else from the press has them yet."

Mel looked surprised. "Come in," he said, flipping up the counter and walking behind it, then holding it for Cesar. "I don't have an office but we can go to the conference room."

They walked through a dark hall and into a room with several long folding tables leaning against a wall that was painted charcoal gray. Four small painted gray tables were pushed together in the middle of the room and Mel grabbed a couple of rolling chairs and brought them to the table. "Have a seat," he said.

"Look," said Cesar. "I want to apologize again for starting off on the wrong foot in my office last week. Also for not getting back to you all the times you called me. I'm sorry. I really am."

Mel just sat, not giving anything away with his expression.

"I have to be honest," went on Cesar. "I'm old school. I'm still understanding the whole online world that's changing under our eyes. Remember, I grew up with newsprint and paper and the seven o'clock news on three channels."

Mel nodded. "I know," he said.

"Right. So you're in the new world. News blogs. I'm sorry," he said again, not quite knowing where to go with it. "I guess I... I didn't get it. I didn't think it was important. It wasn't smart. Or fair. I know better now."

Mel's rigid posture seemed to loosen a little. He hooked his arm around the back of his chair. "You still could have returned my calls."

"I should have. You're right. To be honest, I was holding a grudge."

"A grudge? Why? What for?"

"For the story you dug up about me in my election."

Mel shook his head. "Come again?"

"The story you wrote about my past history years ago."

"I'm still not getting you."

"That old OUI charge you wrote about when I ran for mayor. The headline said I was drinking on duty." Mel still looked confused. "When I was a dog officer."

"The dog officer story?" Mel repeated. "What about it?"

"That story almost killed my campaign."

"But it didn't. Clearly."

"It cost me a lot of votes. And money to hire a lawyer and a PR firm. The lawyer to find old evidence. The PR firm to get it out there in a way people would understand."

"I didn't know all that," said Mel. "I left town right after filing the story. Anyway, I was just doing my job, you know? I was told to find out everything I could about your background. That's what the story was about."

"But the headline was sensationalized. All the other papers ran with it. It made me look unreliable at best, and criminal at worst."

"I didn't write the headline, that happens long after the story is submitted. There's someone else that decides headlines. Now that you mention it, I remember I didn't like it when my mom sent me a copy. Even if I had wanted to, I couldn't have changed a headline. That may sound like I'm passing the buck, but that's the way it was. I'd actually forgotten about it. It wasn't a big deal to me. You won anyway."

Cesar sighed. "I guess we saw it differently."

"For what it's worth, I had no desire to see you lose. I wasn't trying to find any mud. I was just looking for background stuff. Kind of human interest. You caught the dog."

"I did almost lose."

Mel tilted his head and rubbed the back of his neck, then straightened his glasses. "I was doing my job. I can't apologize for that. It was a long time ago, anyway."

"No, I guess you can't." Cesar looked at Mel steadily as if taking his measure. Mel didn't look away. Cesar shrugged. "You know, in my lifetime, it wasn't so long ago."

"I left town right after I wrote that story. Went out to Colorado."

Something had shifted in Mel's tone. Cesar leaned forward a little when he heard it.

"Colorado," Cesar said tentatively. "That's a long way from home."

Mel laughed. "Very true. I spent a winter in Colorado. Then two years in Haiti. Then I came back to start law school."

"Colorado is beautiful, I hear."

"Pretty awesome. I was a snowboard instructor."

"Haiti? That must have been a climate change," said Cesar, carefully.

"Peace Corps," said Mel. "I joined the Peace Corps."

"I always thought I wanted to do that," said Cesar. "I'm impressed. Sorry. Never mind."

Mel laughed awkwardly. "Don't worry about it. I know I get pretty sensitive sometimes."

"So law school next, huh?"

"I started last fall full time. Lived in the city."

"What happened?" asked Cesar.

"No money. Had to move home. Now I commute."

"Oh, I'm sorry. I guess…"

"Don't be. It's not far. Plenty of students do it. Better accommodations than in Haiti. You do what you have to do."

"Ain't that the truth," Cesar said. "So I'm curious. How'd you get started blogging?"

Mel shifted from a casual, sort of draped into his chair position to sitting up tall and looking intensely at Cesar. "I want to make a difference in the world."

"I get that. That's clear," said Cesar. "But why blogging?"

"I started in Haiti. We were lobbying for clean water. To donors. I was blogging about the need, the progress, the results in getting funding for new wells installed. When I got back, I started a blog for the law school. Someone here saw it and hired me to write for their local news feed. They pay me and I take my work seriously."

"Yes, I can see that you do," agreed Cesar. "Look, here." Cesar pulled the papers out, unfolded them, then smoothed them with his hand. He handed them to Mel. "Here's the results of the town vote."

Mel took a quick look at the first page and then flipped it over. "Not very decisive. What's your committee going to do? You said they couldn't agree."

"Here's the interesting part. I told you I wanted diversity on the committee. I've learned that having diverse perspectives is good and it's difficult. I still think I've made the right decision with these choices, however."

"But really, why no developer? No one with real estate experience?"

"That didn't seem important to me," said Cesar. "I wanted people with big picture vision. People who had accomplished things, not to say that couldn't be true of developers. I also didn't want anyone with a pre-determined point of view, someone who might have a conflict of interest. You know?"

"Perhaps. You still don't have consensus," observed Mel. "So what did it get you? Look, you even had to hire that consultant. Consultants never do anything, I hear."

"Really?" said Cesar. "You should meet her. I'd like to introduce her to you if you're interested. I think you'd like her. She's sharp. She's made a real difference in our work. In my leadership," added Cesar.

"Why?" asked Mel, more curious than challenging.

"You know, I'm not exactly sure how she did it," admitted Cesar. "She notices things. How we do things. What we say. She listens carefully. She has a way of listening that's different than the rest of us. You know," he said, musing almost to himself, "we never got taught how to listen. In school I was taught to write, and to read. I took a debate class in high school so in a way I was taught to speak. But no one ever taught me how to listen."

Mel sat quite still, then he shook his head. "Me either. I thought I'd get that in law school. But not so far."

"She asks great questions. Somehow her questions make you find answers in yourself you didn't know were there. Afterwards it seems obvious, but you didn't get there alone. Look," said Cesar, shaking his head as if to bring himself back into the room, into the present. "Speaking of questions, can I ask you a few? It's fine if you say no."

"Shoot," said Mel. "Don't know if I'll have answers, though. Or if I do, if I can share them."

That made Cesar frown. "That's fair, I guess. Obviously, I'm curious about the casino rumor. What do you know?"

"Look. I can't tell you how I know, but you are going to see engineers and architects and land planners poking around town hall within the next three weeks. This is not a rumor."

"But how…?" Cesar leaned forward and then settled back. "You can't tell me how you know, can you?"

"No."

"What can you tell me?"

"There are people in this town who'd like a casino in the area, Mr. Mayor. People my age. Older people. I've talked to them. They're out of work. They want work. People hear that casinos bring jobs and improve property values. You're the mayor. You should know people would want that."

"Look, I don't need you to tell me." Cesar's face was reddening and his shoulder muscles were tensing up. He waited a minute to consider his words. "Look, Mel," he said more quietly, "I want what's best for the people of this town. Based on what you've told me about yourself, I'm guessing you want what's best for this town, too."

Mel nodded.

Cesar shifted to find a more comfortable position. "So we agree. I know people want to get back to work. I know this town needs jobs. I'm against a casino myself but I would consider it, should it become a viable proposal. After all, it did get a significant vote in your precinct, anyway."

"Why are you against it?" asked Mel.

Cesar sighed. "Look at what's happened across the country. There are casinos being built and others failing. How much business is there to go around? What about the folks with the gambling problems? I don't know. Plus if there really is a casino developer for that property, we'll be disqualified for the grant."

"Those are important considerations," agreed Mel. "Can I quote you on that?"

"Look. Sure you can. It's public information. I go to municipal conventions. I listen to other town and state leaders talking about these great hopes for casino revenue, for new jobs. Then a few years later, these same leaders are complaining about casino debt, lost revenue, unrealized taxes. If it seems too good to be true, maybe it is too good to be true. I don't think this town's future should rest on gambling. It doesn't seem right. I'm sorry if that sounds old-fashioned."

Mel sat making notes in his notebook. When he was finished he looked up. "There's still a constituency in town that would like a casino, like the opportunities. What about them?"

Cesar rubbed his hand across his eyes. "Even if they want a casino, it's not up to me to make it happen. I can't propose a casino to the funders of the grant."

"Ah, perhaps not Mr. Mayor. But it would be up to you to broker a deal with the developers. You wouldn't need the grant for that. The town owns the land."

Cesar narrowed his eyes. "What land?"

"Forget it. I shouldn't have said anything," said Mel frowning at his own lapse. He drummed his fingers on the table. "Look, I can't say much but I can tell you this because you'll find it out soon enough. The casino developer isn't looking at the mill building anymore. There wasn't enough parking or enough room for expansion with their hotels and all. The grant money can't go for any other location in town. But the casino is another story. The developers just need locals to demonstrate they are willing."

"So that's why you were pushing the idea of a casino?"

"I was just raising awareness, not necessarily pushing it. I do think it could be really good for the town."

"Seemed a lot like pushing," said Cesar.

"Blogging is personal opinion. It's not the same as straight news. So I have more leeway. But listen. Any one of those three proposals you've got could be good for the town."

"Well, I'm glad you think that way," said Cesar.

"Which is it going to be, Mayor?"

"Hopefully, I'll have an answer in a few days."

"Can I call you?" asked Mel quickly.

"By all means," said Cesar. "And I'll take your call or call you right back."

Nancy Hardaway

Pause and Reflect

Chapter 46

Julia's phone rang. It was Mark.

"Can you stop by my clinic later? I have something for you," he said.

Julia arrived at the clinic after it had closed and Mark was waiting at the door for her with a plant wrapped in florist paper in his arms.

"This is to show you my appreciation for your help," said Mark.

"How lovely," said Julia, starting to take it from him.

"No, wait. I'd like you to see it. I picked it carefully," he said. "Come back to the kitchen with me." They walked through to the kitchen and Mark put the plant on the table. "Open it," he urged.

Julia carefully opened the paper. Inside was a perfect miniature rose bush, covered with lush ruby red blooms.

"I wanted something that would show you I really learned something from you. I picked a plant because I thought it represented natural cycles things go through, and change is sort of like that. I picked a rose bush because of the thorns, you know, the need to be tough at times. What do you think?"

"How could I not love it?" she said. "What a thoughtful gift."

"Wait, there's more. I want to show you something," said Mark, grinning. "I've been working hard to learn how to say no. I cheated, though."

"What? How? What do you mean, cheated?"

"I didn't start with my office staff. I experimented with my dog," he said, opening the door to the storeroom. Julia instinctively took a step back. "Say hello to Muldoon," said Mark, as the dog bounded out of the room. "Slow down, fella. Sit."

The dog looked up in surprise and hesitated. Mark moved in front of Julia and crossed his arms and the dog crouched but didn't quite get its butt onto the floor. Mark waited and finally the dog gave up and sank to the ground, laying down and dropping his nose between his legs.

"Good boy!" Mark said in a calm voice and stepped aside. Muldoon stayed where he was.

Julia looked from Mark to the dog. "I'm impressed!"

"An improvement, right? You know, when he was a puppy I trained him to sit and come and all that. You could probably figure out that I was lax about enforcing the commands. I'd say sit, then repeat it and repeat it and repeat it and sometimes he'd sit and sometimes I'd just give up. I've been practicing for the last two weeks."

"Hmmmm," Julia said. "Do you have your staff sitting on command as well? They're going to hate me."

Mark laughed. "Absolutely, wait 'til you see them. If they were here I'd open the door and yell 'come' so they could say hello." They laughed together.

"So obviously things are going better," said Julia.

Mark nodded. "First I told them they had no choice. This was something we'd have to figure out together. I arranged for some evening review sessions with the software training team and provided Red Tankard beer and gourmet pizzas. I paid for child care for anyone who wanted to attend. Then I got the head of the state hospital association to review the history and rationale behind the regulations. I even pulled a favor and got an old med school buddy to come in for a lunch meeting. Scott's a well known and highly respected author on health care quality issues and had written about the benefits of well-designed electronic health records. Getting someone else to answer their questions has really helped."

Julia nodded. "Sounds quite thorough."

"You know, even this morning, I noticed that one of the nurses and the doc who was the last hold out were sitting by a computer working away together."

Julia looked out at Muldoon, who'd fallen asleep. "I like to hear about progress," she said.

"I've been getting to know my clerical staff, too. You know, I am really lucky. I have great people out there."

"It doesn't surprise me," said Julia. "If you hadn't, you probably would have been forced to get to know them better before this."

"I hadn't thought of it that way, but you're right. I'm actually enjoying getting to know them. They had some real legitimate issues with the software, too. We're getting some improvements made now."

"That's great, Mark," said Julia.

"And I can't believe the difference with the medical team. But what really mattered was getting them involved in the implementation. Them figuring out their own learning and adoption process. Their ideas were much better than mine!"

"Maybe. After all, they know where they are on the learning curve more than you do. You gave them some control, within limits. That helps, too."

"I should know that from my work with patients. When they have more control of their treatment path, they're more successful. I don't know why I didn't see it the same way."

"Well, now you do," said Julia simply.

"So thank you," said Mark, helping Julia re-wrap the plant. "You coming to the meeting tomorrow? Redley and Fletcher are bringing back their findings."

"I wouldn't miss it," she said.

Nancy Hardaway

Pause and Reflect

Chapter 47

The Blue Ribbon Committee gathered in the conference room with the mayor at one end of the long scarred table and Redley sitting down at the other end. They reviewed the data that Fletcher had provided and it appeared that the idea of creating a community center, with a performing arts hall, and a business incubator could potentially be financially feasible and meet the conditions of the grant in terms of sustainability. Redley had met with the architects and they felt that some combination of space would be possible.

"They said they obviously couldn't come up with a design this quickly, but..." she reached into her briefcase slowly. "Here's what they came up with."

She took out a roll of yellow tissue and unrolled it across the table. There were various sketches of the mill building's exterior and interior floor plans. "They started talking with one another, got excited, pulled out this roll of paper and started sketching. They forgot I was there until I said I had to go so they told me to take this. They want it back, though. I figured you'd all want to see it."

The others all stood and leaned over the drawings.

Fletcher pointed to one sketch. "Look at this. I love the way they've created the modular stage with the practice rooms around it. And is this a moveable wall?" He pointed to a zigzag across the back of the auditorium.

"Yes!" exclaimed Mark. "Look at this. They've put the big exercise room right behind it so it could be opened up and create more seating for bigger concerts. Here's a note that suggests folding bleacher type seating would tuck up against the walls."

"I like the common courtyard area in the middle," said Cesar. "They've opened it right through the building so it looks right out at the river. It can be a lobby, or a meeting space."

225

"Is this a running track?" asked Mark, pointing to a double line that ran around the inside of the courtyard. He turned toward Redley who had walked away from the table and was looking out the window. She came back and joined them.

"What they're talking about is kind of like a catwalk space that would be a running or walking track overlooking the courtyard. They said it would be in keeping with the history of the mill building because there used to be catwalks for the managers to watch over all the workers."

"Oh, look here," said Fletcher, his fingers traveling across the yellow tissue. "Here's a long wall marked gallery space. That will be great."

"Where's the incubator space?" asked Cesar, suddenly.

"They said it wouldn't all fit," said Redley, in a flat tone. "It was their professional opinion that the incubator didn't really fit the other two uses that well anyway."

Everyone turned toward Redley. She sat down again at the end of the table. "So this is what they came up with."

Cesar looked over to Julia and back to Redley. "I can see you're upset."

"Disappointed. Really disappointed."

Cesar sighed. Fletcher and Mark sat back down in their seats.

"So what would you like to see us do, Redley?" asked Cesar. "I must say, I'm disappointed, too, but I'd like to hear what you think we should do before I propose anything."

Redley's face was hidden by her hair as she looked down at her hands. She shrugged and took a deep breath. "Let's go with this plan. We don't have time. It will be good for the town. Maybe I can do something about the incubator with my own business somehow."

"Now wait a minute," said Mark. "We need a unanimous decision. Seems to me they could squeeze in some office space there."

"A little corner wouldn't really do it. You need enough space to build a viable business energy in the building. Plus money for technical support." Redley shook her head.

"They're probably right. Your two ideas need a lot of square footage. They're for public use. Offices don't complement the public uses that well, anyway."

"Fletcher," said Cesar. "What do you think?"

Fletcher took off his glasses. "I think they're probably right. On the other hand, I've gotten really interested in Redley's idea. I think it's a good one for the town."

"All right," said Cesar. "I agree. Let's try to widen our focus. We all agree that all three uses are good for the town. The town agreed as well. The experts say all three can't fit in the building. Is there another possibility we've overlooked?"

They sat silently looking over the plans in front of them. The clock ticked away.

"I'm thinking of all these other empty buildings on Main Street," said Cesar, finally.

Fletcher sat up, tapping his glasses on his palm. "I wonder...."

"What?" asked Mark and Cesar together.

"I can't promise anything, but I had a thought. Redley, would you be willing to come talk to my bank board about your idea?"

She shrugged. "I guess, but why?"

"Just an idea. Maybe we could put some of our foreclosed buildings to use temporarily, with some help from the Economic Development Board."

Redley leaned forward. "Really? You think?"

"I make no promises and we'd have a long road ahead, figuring it out," said Fletcher.

"Maybe the regional Chamber of Commerce could help," said Cesar.

Redley took a deep breath. "Look guys, I appreciate you trying to make me feel better, but really, our decision about the grant needs to come first."

"It's not about making you feel better," said Mark. "What's best for this town? We need the kind of jobs and new companies you're talking about. Even I can see it now."

"I've got someone who might be able to connect us with some angel investors," added Fletcher. "When I happened to bring up the idea to one of our bigger commercial clients, he mentioned he had some connections that could be interested if we went forward with it. I'll set up a meeting with him as well. It's a long shot, but shall we try it?"

"Maybe we could have a retail and hospitality focus if we'll be on Main Street," Redley said, energized with ideas. "Should we put the tech folks upstairs, maybe, since they don't need visibility, except virtually?"

They spent a few more minutes exploring ways to support a business incubator, before Cesar brought them back to the decision on the mill building. They reviewed all the rest of the sketches with lots of questions, but nothing significant came up.

"I say we vote," said Redley, then looked at Julia, who had opened her mouth as if to speak. "Or maybe I'll say I'm ready to vote, but we should make sure everyone's questions are answered."

Chapter 48

"Okay folks, let's take a moment to check in," said Cesar, "before we jump into this final decision process." Redley started to roll up the plans but Cesar stopped her. "No, that's okay. Leave them out where we can see them when we're ready. Fletcher, as our committee's oldest resident, well not oldest, but living in town the longest, you know. Anyway, Fletcher, you first. What do you think of this?"

Fletcher picked up his spreadsheets, neatened them, then put them back down squarely in front of him. "I like it," he said. "I like where we've gotten. I think there are things we have to be careful about. There's a little bit more risk here than I'd prefer. But on balance, I like it." He nodded. "Especially if we can also make Redley's incubator happen."

"Okay, how about you, Mark, as another long time resident?" asked Cesar.

"I like the plan. I like the way all the ideas are woven together. I like the way we brought the town into it. It was a hard process, but I'm glad we stuck with it. I really think this combination is going to bring this town back and I think they'll all be behind it. I'm thrilled."

"I guess that leaves me," said Redley. "This is something we can all be proud of that will change the future. There were times I have to say I hated being on this committee, I'm not a good committee person, I can see that. I'm still disappointed we couldn't fit everything in, but I'm totally with this plan. Okay?"

Everyone nodded.

"What about you, Chief?" Redley asked the mayor.

"I am in total agreement. I agree with what you've all stated so let's take action. We have a vote to take right now, for the record. Will someone make a motion to adopt this plan as our grant proposal?"

"So moved," said Fletcher.

"Second," said Redley.

"Any discussion?" asked the mayor. "Here's your last chance to advocate." He waited. "Hearing none, I'll call the question. All those in favor say aye."

All three voices around the table said aye, and Cesar added his in after he heard the others.

"That carries unanimously, as required by the grant conditions," he exclaimed. "People, you did it! Congratulations!"

Julia started to clap and they all joined her enthusiastically.

"One more thing," said Redley. "Chief, you've been great to work with. A really good leader. I appreciate how much space you gave us. Particularly now I'm more aware of working at that in my own company. So thank you."

"I'd like to say the same, Mayor," said Fletcher. "I've known you a long time, voted for you, even though you're not my party affiliation. But working with you gives me a greater appreciation for why I'll vote for you again."

"I agree," said Mark. "You sure have my vote."

"Thank you all, both for thinking it and saying it. I really mean that," said Cesar. He turned to Julia. "But I think Julia, here, deserves a lot of credit."

"Yes, that's true," said Fletcher. "I know you all thought I'd never say this, but thank you, Julia."

"Yes," said Mark and Redley in unison.

"You certainly have developed as a team," said Julia, grinning.

"Oh, is that an understatement," said Redley, rolling her eyes. "I don't even like to think about where we were when you arrived." She looked around the table.

"I think I speak for all of us," said Cesar, "when I say we got more than we expected from you, Julia." He raised one eyebrow seriously, then laughed heartily.

"I don't know whether to take that as a compliment or not," said Julia.

"Yes you do," said Cesar, and they both laughed. "I've gotten to know you well enough to know that."

"Well then, I'll give you a compliment back. You all were open and willing to try new things."

"Not me!" said Fletcher. "Not at first. But you converted even me."

"Huh. We were desperate. That's why," said Mark with a laugh. "But seriously, is this is the last time Julia will be with us as a team?"

Both Cesar and Julia nodded in unison. "We have work to do to complete the grant but our funds have run out and Julia thinks we're ready to graduate, anyway."

"Then we should do that evaluate part she's told us about," said Mark. "Let's talk about what we each learned through this process. How about it?"

"We could be here forever," said Cesar, seriously. "But it's a good idea so I'll start, and keep it brief. I learned I have a good instinct for putting a team together. That four people working hard can get good things done."

"Come on, Chief," said Redley, poking him with her pencil. "You can do better than that. We were working hard before Julia came and we weren't getting things done."

"True. Okay, let me try again." He steepled his fingers and leaned back in his chair. "The first thing I learned from you, Julia, was that being a mayor is harder than being police chief because I can't carry a gun."

Everyone chuckled.

He pursed his lips. "Julia showed me a lot about true leadership, about influence. I don't know quite how to put it into words, though. Oh yeah, and that you can't force people to trust you."

"Indeed," responded Julia. "You learned that the hard way with Mr. Schroom. You did turn him around though, right?"

"To some extent. I think that happened when I started to imagine what it was like from his point of view."

"You started to get curious," said Julia. "It started inside."

"I guess I'd agree," said Cesar. "I think that's what happened with this team, here, right?" They all nodded, then got quiet. The clock ticked in the background.

"Is that it?" asked Redley.

"No, not really but that's all I can think of right now," said Cesar. "No, wait. Also how being a leader isn't always about doing. Sometimes it's about just getting out of the way. I sure saw that with this team right at the end, here." He nodded. "Now someone else go."

"That's a good one for me to tag onto," said Redley. "That getting out of the way thing is something I'm having to work on. To be a better leader, I have to let go. I thought I was but I wasn't. Still not very good at it but Julia's helping me. Yeah, and to solve problems for people isn't helping them as much as I thought. I need to let them learn how to solve their own problems and find better ways to use my time."

Mark chimed in. "Important for me to remember, too. I've had to get people more involved in their own solutions. Life isn't always about diagnose and prescribe."

"You know, Mark," said Redley, "That's exactly what I was doing. Diagnosing the problem and prescribing the solution. I was trying so hard to keep my people from failing that I was holding them back."

"But you were good at supporting them, right?" asked Mark.

Redley shrugged. "I guess that's what Julia would say, right? So I'll keep supporting them, especially when they screw up. With my giving them more leeway, though, they've already come up with some great new ideas."

"You know, innovation does take risk," Julia said thoughtfully.

"Don't talk about risk to a banker," said Fletcher.

"So what did you learn, Fletch?" asked Redley.

"For me it's sort of the opposite. You said you were holding people back. I was pushing too hard. I think that's one of the things I learned," said Fletcher. "What did you say, Julia? To start with, where people are? I think I'm starting to get that. To not just push on to where I want them to be. You called it a paradox, Julia, and that's exactly what it is."

"Wait a minute," asked Redley. "That doesn't sound like the situation with your assistant."

Fletcher nodded. "No, that's the connection piece the mayor just mentioned. With my assistant and even some of the people on my senior team... I'm noticing more. I've caught a few issues before they became worse. So that's good. That other was more about my son. I wish I was doing as well with him. We're getting along better but his behavior hasn't changed."

"Be patient," suggested Julia. "That's good advice with any teenager. They're constantly changing."

"That's my cue," said Mark. "Change. You'd think I'd get it. I watch it daily in my practice. Kids grow up. People get old. It's constant. But I didn't get how it worked in organizations."

"Do you get it now?" asked Fletcher. "I think that's one we all deal with constantly."

Mark shrugged. "I won't be getting an A in the course. But that cycle Julia drew for us really stuck with me. The mountain diagram. The way work gets done. Whatever you call it, that natural progression of things. Paying attention, like Fletcher said, but paying attention to where I am as a leader versus where the others in my organization are. I really get that now. And I understand that people's resistance to change isn't just to wreck my day. It's their biological mechanism," said Mark to the others. "The organism's systemic response. That resonates with the scientist in me."

They all nodded.

"It's funny," added Mark. "I asked Julia to help me with my medical and admin staff, but I'm finding myself using it with my patients, too. And I'm learning to say no."

They all sat quietly for a minute.

"Wait," said Redley. "We can't forget the importance of asking questions. Me of all people. Isn't that important to you all?" she asked looking around the table with a grin. "Those three rules for good teamwork, remember? Like birds flocking? Right, Julia?"

"Wait a minute," Cesar said, as he jumped up and opened the closet in the corner of the room. As he rustled around they all watched curiously. "Here it is," he mumbled from behind a box. He came out with a flip chart and turned it all to face them with a look of triumph. "I kept that original chart that Julia had me write on. Questions, Sharing Time, Focusing the Lens. Remember?"

Julia burst out laughing. "A collector's item, now."

"One more thing about questions," said Redley, looking at the chart thoughtfully. "It's that balance again. I'm trying to think about those two words—inquiry and what was the opposite?"

"You mean advocacy?" answered Fletcher.

Redley nodded. "Right. Inquiry and advocacy. I know I'm paying a lot of attention to that. We all figured out we're very good at advocating, didn't we?"

"You all are, and should stay that way," said Cesar. "Remember? Julia said it's about adding. Don't stop doing what you do well, just add to your choices. So, yes. Ask questions, but don't give up your advocating. You'll need to be strong advocates for this facility all around town."

"We'll have to ask questions of people around town, too," said Mark. "What features they'd like to see. That sort of detail."

Cesar nodded. "You know that reminds me of those community meetings we planned. Mark mentioned the cycle but he didn't mention how we applied it to those meetings. I've used it in lots of other meetings since them. I think I've had some of the best meetings ever when I pay attention to that cycle. What were the stages? No wait, don't tell me. Awareness, engagement," he ticked off on his fingers. "Then there's analysis and planning, then action. And last but very important is evaluation. There, I got them all!"

"You did indeed, Mayor," said Julia. "You've all worked through a full cycle together and here you are at evaluation."

"You know," said Mark thoughtfully "Maybe we should consider another round of meetings with the new plan."

"What a great idea!" said Cesar. "People should see this. They'll want to see it. We need to get their buy-in and build excitement. Get them engaged."

"Just let me know. I'll make sure to have Angie fit them into my schedule," said Fletcher. "What about you, Redley? We still need you!"

"I'm in," said Redley. "As soon as we get final drawings from the architects."

They were all silent for a minute.

"You know," said Redley, pushing her hair back over her shoulders with a shrug and sitting up. "Everything we've all mentioned is really useful but I just realized something important."

The tone of Redley's voice made everyone turn to look at her. She held their attention quietly for a moment.

"I think what has made the biggest impression on me is Julia's presence." She turned to face Julia. "You're so present. That sounds silly in a way, but so important." She took a deep breath and tilted her head first one way then another as she frowned at Julia. "Let me see how to say this. Presence, your impact on me, is how present you are to me, for me. You're right there, Julia. Totally. You're not lost on some other thought, or what you want to say next. You never miss what's going on in us. You notice so much. And you just notice. You don't sit in judgment. That statement you made once about believing that people are doing the best they can. Your optimistic stance. The appreciation and lack of judgment. That doesn't just sit in your head. It projects out. I just can feel it. It makes a difference."

"You know, you're right," said Mark. "I don't think I realized it until you just started talking about it."

"Well, it's real hard to articulate it clearly but I sure feel it," said Redley. "I think the other things we've talked about are sort of skills or behaviors I've learned. New ways of looking at things. They're great and important, and have and will make my life as a leader, actually my life in general, easier. I'll be more effective. But this presence thing. This is not about doing. It's about being. It's how you are in the world."

Fletcher and Cesar both nodded slowly.

"That's it exactly," said Mark. "I'm glad you put it into words, Redley."

"That's very nice to hear," said Julia. "It is. I love what I do and I'm thrilled it makes a difference. You've all allowed me to make a difference. You've been open to learning, to making it yours. Both the process and the content. Right from the beginning you've had a clear vision of where you've wanted this town to be in the future. Different ways to get there but a shared vision, even when you didn't realize it. You've gone out and found the town shares it as well. Now you've got a chance to make it happen."

"Julia," said Cesar. "We couldn't have done it without you."

"I look forward to the grand opening of the restored building," Julia said. "You will invite me, won't you?"

"You bet!" said Cesar. He grinned and stood, and the rest of them stood as well. "Somehow I don't think this is the last any of us will be working with Julia, though this contract is done."

"I'll be working with her for a while," said Redley as she started to roll up the sketches then stopped abruptly. "Wait a minute, Chief. I wonder if you've heard any more news?"

"On what?" said Cesar with a frown.

"The casino!" answered Redley. "What about the casino? What happened about that?"

Cesar nodded. "Actually, my staff confirmed that the casino operators quickly stopped looking at the mill building because there wasn't enough parking. They're looking at that large parcel across the river right now. It may turn out that since they've seen there's so little appetite for it in town, they'll just decide to go elsewhere. At least that's my hope, but you never know."

"Interesting," said Redley.

Cesar grinned. "It ain't over til it's over, as they say. Okay, we've got this step done. Again, thank you all for your hard work. Now we start a new cycle. We have to finish writing the grant."

With the final grant proposal review meeting scheduled, the Blue Ribbon Committee said goodbye, and went their separate ways.

Cesar walked Julia out of the town hall and down to her car. Daffodils were poking up from the ground in a sunny spot on the corner.

"I wasn't sure you were the right person when I saw you, Julia. You know I had my doubts. But you turned out to be exactly what we needed."

"You know, Cesar, you probably could have gotten here if you'd had enough time. I don't think of what I do as adding something completely new. I think of it as helping people and teams and organizations to reach their full potency, their full power. With less time and less work expended. Helping you find the answers that are already inside you."

"That, my dear lady, is exactly what you did. Do you have a name for it?"

They had come to a stop in front of Julia's sports car.

"Potentiation is what I like to call it. It's a word from chemistry. You hear it in pharmaceuticals where one substance makes another more powerful. Like caffeine with aspirin. I just try to partner with you to make you stronger."

"So we were the headache, and you were the caffeine?" Cesar said, chuckling.

"Something like that, Mayor," said Julia, smiling. "It's what you and Redley and the rest do with your own people."

"I think this could be our legacy," he said. "Don't you think?"

Pause and Reflect

APPENDIX A

Chapter Summary

To provide an easy way for you to find and reread or discuss the individual lessons in the book with colleagues or with your team, each chapter's main idea along with a snippet of the action is provided below.

Chapter 1: **Work with differences:** There are both advantages and disadvantages when people work together from very varied backgrounds, either by culture, or experience, or technical knowledge that develops within organizational silos. The pros are the diversity of perspectives and potential for creative options, the cons are the conflicts that may develop. Cesar is frustrated by the challenges of working with his team of people whose different backgrounds and opinions have them stuck in conflict. (*pp. 1-4*)

Chapter 2: **See what's working well:** Development and improvement for individuals, teams, and organizations happens most successfully when it starts on a foundation of exploring strengths and competencies. This team is good at advocating for their opinions. Because it has become such a prominent behavior, it has taken over their meetings. They need to become curious about each perspective and start asking questions. (*pp. 5-8*)

Chapter 3: **Use three rules for more effective team behavior:** Teams work more effectively when all the participants practice three behaviors—asking questions, participating equally by taking their share of time, and shifting their focus from big picture to detail and from the group to their own interior responses. This team benefits from adding what they are completely lacking. Their time is spent advocating and they need to add the opposite, which is inquiry—asking questions. (*pp. 9-16*)

Chapter 4: **Avoid getting stuck in default behaviors:** Leaders develop strategies and behaviors that work well for them and support their success over the years. Sometimes these strategies and behaviors become so ingrained that they become a default, occurring automatically and without choice. Each of the three leaders has a specific behavior pattern that may sometimes serve them well but gets in their way when it is overused. (*pp. 17-22*)

Chapter 5: **Build effective working relationships:** Effectively working with others takes a foundation of trust and awareness. Fletcher is a results-oriented businessman who understands the need for that foundation of trust with customers but now needs to understand the importance of taking time to build a relationship with his staff in order to work effectively with them. (*pp. 23-28*)

Chapter 6: **Begin meetings well:** Good meetings have natural cycles. A meeting, whether between two people or many, is more efficient and successful when it has a well-crafted beginning. Good beginnings include time for the participants to connect with one another and understand a framework of the purpose and content of the meeting. Cesar is under stress for results and in such a hurry that he just wants to jump into the work. (*pp. 29-32*)

Chapter 7: **Stay open to resistance:** Resistance occurs when someone doesn't want what you want, for whatever the reason. Reacting to the emotion caused by resistance is rarely effective, and instead often has the opposite effect—of fanning the flames, or causing escalating defensiveness. Staying open and getting interested and curious is the far more effective (albeit challenging) response that Julia demonstrates in response to the mayor's anger. (*pp. 33-38*)

Chapter 8: **End meetings and conversations well:** The natural cycle of a meeting or a conversation includes a complete ending. A good ending includes time to clarify and reiterate what has occurred during the meeting—a decision or next steps, etc.—because too often people leave with dramatically different assumptions. Good endings also include a moment to evaluate the work accomplished together. Julia helps the group notice their progress and their sense of satisfaction. (*pp. 39-42*)

Chapter 9: **Lean in and ask questions:** The impact of getting curious in the face of resistance is significant. Cesar goes home and relates the saga of Julia's response to his anger, realizing how her behavior calmed him and allowed him to proceed with the meeting. He also shares the positive impact of the team's use of questions. (*pp. 43-48*)

Chapter 10: **Rebuild trust:** When trust is eroded in a working relationship (or any relationship), specific action is needed to rebuild it. Julia attends to the breach in her relationship with Cesar by addressing the problem quickly and directly rather than hoping it will blow over. She builds trust by connecting with him from the heart—human being to human being, rather than consultant to client—noticing the family photos and sharing a bit of herself. (*pp. 49-50*)

Chapter 11: **Refocus your lens:** Good work requires that you learn how to see the big picture and see the details, shifting your attention rapidly back and forth and noticing patterns. Julia uses the metaphor of a dance to explain how Cesar can shift from detail to big picture and start to become more aware of the patterns in his team's behavior. (*p. 51-52*)

Chapter 12: **Start where you are:** Change starts where you are, so you need to pay close attention to the current situation before you try to move forward. This applies equally to personal change and large organizational change. Julia shares the example of Alcoholics Anonymous to help Cesar understand the concept of encouraging the team to explore the current conditions in town to help them decide on changes. (*pp. 53-54*)

Chapter 13: **Choose your response to emotion:** When people get emotional, you are more effective if you can get interested and choose how to respond, rather than simply react from your own emotional default. Julia explains to the team why she intentionally chose to respond to Cesar's earlier anger in a way that wouldn't escalate his lack of trust in her. (*pp. 55-62*)

Chapter 14: **Lead change intentionally:** Change occurs through a sequence of steps that involve understanding the problem, investigating solutions, and moving into action. Leaders of change progress through these steps first and then move to action, leaving the rest of their team in their wake. Julia helps Mark notice how long he's been involved in the change effort at his clinic prior to involving his staff. (*pp. 63-68*)

Chapter 15: **Appreciate why people resist change:** What we call resistance is a natural way for people to slow things down, like brakes in a car. They may have different information than you, they may not see the benefit of the change, and they may not like or trust the agent of change (you or your organization.) Through Julia's questions, Mark starts to explore the different reasons his staff may be resisting the changes he's instituting, and opportunities to help them through it. (*pp. 69-72*)

Chapter 16: **Lead through influence:** Leaders sometimes have the power and authority of a positional title in the hierarchy, but informal leadership can occur anywhere in an organization, or "from any seat in the house." What leadership requires is the ability to influence. Julia and the team discuss their perspectives on leadership and how to build followership. (*pp. 73-76*)

Chapter 17: Slow down and choose behaviors under stress:
We naturally default to the tried and true when we are under
stress. The brain, when it experiences threat, shuts down the
pre-frontal cortex, which is where new learning and openness
is possible. So time pressure or other stress can momentarily
erase new behaviors we're learning. Julia intervenes as she
sees the team jump back to their pattern of advocacy when
they feel threatened by the idea of a casino in town. She
encourages them to slow down so they can choose how they
want to react and how they want to behave, rather than shift
into their default. (*pp. 77-80*)

Chapter 18: Build support: Part of building support for
change is keeping people involved in the process. If you
were leading a hike, you wouldn't climb up alone, leaving
everyone in the parking lot, then ask them to follow later.
Mark helps the team see that they need to involve the town in
the change process for the mill building. (*pp. 81-86*)

Chapter 19: Scan your team to stay aware: Teams work
better when they, and particularly their leader, have the
ability to observe both *what* they get done and *how* they are
doing. Julia reminds Cesar to use the observation skills he
developed as a police officer in his leadership, taking time
to scan the faces, energy, and body language of the people
at the table, especially when making a decision. (*pp. 87-88*)

**Chapter 20: Attend to the difference between intent and
impact:** Paying attention to how your behavior impacts
people is a crucial leadership skill, as is the ability to respond
to people in a way that is meaningful to them. Fletcher
realizes that his attempts to compliment his assistant went
awry because they were delivered in a way that made her
uncomfortable. (*pp. 89-90*)

Chapter 21: Break down silos: Creating spaces and
opportunities for people of different disciplines to connect

can break down the walls between them and lead to innovation. Redley presents her ideas for a business incubator that builds on the best practices of building creative connections, and explains why she's a brewer. (*pp. 91-96*)

Chapter 22: **Share personal history and vulnerability:** Leaders are most influential when they are willing to share why things are important to them, and when they are willing to be vulnerable. Mark explains how his personal tragedy and the support he received from the town has led him to value a community center. (*pp. 97-102*)

Chapter 23: **Understand leadership boundaries of responsibility and accountability:** In making decisions, leaders can go it alone, can solicit input and opinions but reserve the final decision, they can pursue a consensus decision in which all agree, or they can go for a majority opinion. The team discusses how to manage the input of the town, and Julia cautions them to make clear which kind of decision they will be making. (*pp. 103-106*)

Chapter 24: **Scan for content and process:** In any interaction there is content (the issue you are discussing) and process (the way you are discussing or interacting around that content). A leader needs to learn to pay attention to both content and process, whether participating in a conversation or viewing the entire purpose of the organization and the culture through which work gets done. It is very easy to get so interested in content that you lose focus on process. Even Julia can be seduced by interesting content, momentarily stepping out of her role of adding a focus on process to the team. (*pp. 107-112*)

Chapter 25: **Learn successful team behavior:** Three behaviors that help teams function successfully are asking questions of one another, each person taking their fair share of time and responsibility, and shifting focus from detail to big picture and from oneself to the others. Noticing what helps successful work is as important as noticing what gets in the way, and Julia points out how well the team works when they are all making use of the three behaviors of asking questions, sharing time, and refocusing. (*pp. 113-118*)

Chapter 26: **Acknowledge current reality:** The more you try to push someone to change, the more you may encounter their resistance. Julia suggests that if Fletcher starts by accepting his son's interests, paradoxically changes might occur in their relationship and even in his son's interests. (*pp. 119-122*)

Chapter 27: **Examine your part in every interaction:** Relationships are created by the behavior of both people, in spite of how easy it is to blame the other when things go badly. Cesar's wife encourages him to examine how his own actions might be contributing to Mel Schroom's behavior. (*pp. 123-126*)

Chapter 28: **Develop skills in others:** A leader's crucial role is developing their people, and to do that they need to foster problem solving rather than offer solutions. Redley's desire to support her people and prevent failure is interfering in their professional growth, as well as her company's capacity for expansion. (*pp. 127-136*)

Chapter 29: **Ask, don't tell:** Because leaders' experiences and position in their organization gives them deep and detailed knowledge and because they are often so focused on results, they can be quick to jump into action and solve problems. Redley's action orientation plays out in her constant problem solving for her people and Julia encourages her to slow down that process through questions, both of herself and others. Throughout the book we see Julia modeling this skill of asking questions that invite exploration and discovery rather than providing instant answers. (*pp. 137-138*)

Chapter 30: **Assume people are doing their best:** Trying to appreciate why people behave the way they do allows you to understand their behavior and step beyond your immediate default judgments to give you more choices. Cesar's assumption that Schroom is just a jerk is getting in his way of figuring out how to respond more effectively. (*pp. 139-144*)

Chapter 31: **Examine your assumptions:** Your assumptions about yourself, about the issue, and about the other person will determine your behavior. They'll get in your way if you don't acknowledge them as assumptions, and examine them rather than treat them as fact. Julia encourages Cesar to hold his assumptions lightly and to get curious about how Schroom's motives might be different than they appear. (*pp. 145-146*)

Chapter 32: **Be intentional about your presence:** Everyone needs to pay attention to how they impact people, and particularly leaders whose presence is more potent because of their role. Cesar needs to examine what kind of an impact he wants to make with Schroom, so his choices of where and how they meet support that intention. (*pp. 147-150*)

Chapter 33: **Know your role:** Seeing the larger context, defining vision, encouraging participation and accepting accountability are all part of leadership. The team questions each other about how they see themselves as leaders, and determines how they want to define their team role in leading the town on a decision about the use of the mill building. (*pp. 151-154*)

Chapter 34: **Complete a natural cycle of work:** There are five phases to a natural cycle of how work gets done, both individually and collectively: awareness, engagement, mobilization, action, and evaluation. Paying attention to this cycle helps you create conversations, meetings and projects that generate momentum and achieve results. The team plans the community meetings to successfully complete each phase of the natural cycle. (*pp. 155-160*)

Chapter 35: **Influence others through preparation, presence, and presentations**: Preparation of your presence is as important as preparing your content when you want to influence, or sell a product, idea, or your service. Redley explains her sales process as the team decides how they want to prepare themselves for the meetings, including choices of what they wear, how they think, how they pace their speeches, and how they stand on stage. (*pp. 161-166*)

Chapter 36: **Learn to say no:** Part of the loneliness of leadership is the need to hold people accountable, learning how to say no and how to disappoint people at times. While Mark needs to explore the resistance he is encountering from his staff, he also needs to learn to expand his behavior choices beyond his desire to please. (*pp. 167-172*)

Chapter 37: **Evaluate your work**: Taking time to evaluate is a crucial part of the work process, leading to important learning and improvements. Evaluation needs to start with noticing and appreciating what worked well to create a firm foundation on which to build. Julia encourages the team to take time at the close of their first community meeting to evaluate their success as well as areas for improvement. (*pp. 173-180*)

Chapter 38: **Connect before acting:** Interactions are far more successful when there is some honest level of connection between the people, based on genuine interest and appreciation. Julia draws Cesar's attention to notice how his appreciation of the team had an impact, and encourages him to connect with Schroom before moving into action when they meet. (*pp. 181-182*)

Chapter 39: **Go slow to go fast:** When situations are sensitive or volatile, often going slow is more effective than jumping to action. Cesar manages his own angry response to Schroom's blog and encourages the team to move slowly and learn more before they take action. (*pp. 183-186*)

Chapter 40: **Delegate:** In order to focus their attention on what only they can do, leaders all have to determine what to delegate and how to delegate. The process requires being willing to step away from detail and allow others room to experiment, to succeed, fail, and grow. Redley has tracked her pattern of relating to staff and recognizes she needs to delegate responsibility by establishing clarity of boundaries and information flow. (*pp. 187-190*)

Chapter 41: **Balance relational and strategic behaviors:** Each situation and each interaction requires a different combination of finding opportunities to relate and getting things done. The nuances of behaviors and their meaning vary for each person, and leaders need to be sensitive to balancing their impact and the expectations of others. Cesar's awkward persistence in trying to relate personally to Schroom backfires and gets in the way of mutual respect or trust. (*pp. 191-196*)

Chapter 42: **Look from the other point of view:** When interactions don't go well, it's important to pay attention to the details and perspectives of both parties, particularly when trying to build trust. Julia helps Cesar gain perspective by asking questions that allow him to begin to see the situation from Schroom's point of view, both in terms of their shared past and in terms of their unsuccessful meeting. (*pp. 197-202*)

Chapter 43: **Connect quickly:** Leaders can use simple opportunities to build connection with their staff. Some leaders do it instinctively, having seen such behavior modeled at work or at home. Other leaders have to work harder to notice and take advantage of the opportunities to build relationships, as Fletcher does in this scene when he greets his staff as he enters in the morning rather than just heading for his desk, and when he remembers and engages his assistant about her daughter's upcoming event. (*pp. 203-204*)

Chapter 44: **Lead a high-performing team:** The role of a leader changes as the team learns how to work together. Compared to early stages of team development when the leader has to be very active, as the team starts to perform seamlessly the leader's role becomes less central and more focused on support, providing resources and encouragement as necessary. (*pp. 205-212*)

Chapter 45: **Build trust through openness:** The requirement for building trust is creating a sense of safety and comfort. In coming to see Mel Schroom in his own surroundings and starting their meeting by apologizing, Cesar creates a more comfortable environment that allows Mel to be less defensive and more open. (*pp. 213-220*)

Chapter 46: **Engage with change:** People become more willing to change when they are held accountable and have some measure of participation and can have some measure of participation and control in the process. Mark knows this lesson from his work with his patients and successfully applies it to his role as a leader in his clinic. (*pp. 221-224*)

Chapter 47: **Maintain inclusion:** Decisions and conclusions are rarely perfect for everyone, and leaders need to find ways to include those whose opinions and choices may not have been selected. When Redley's option for the mill building doesn't fit with the others, the team maintains their unity by addressing the issue directly, noticing and verifying her response, and exploring other options. (*pp. 225-228*)

Chapter 48: **Articulate lessons learned:** The process of learning is reinforced when you have to articulate to others what is meaningful about the learning. It is the last step in the natural cycle of work and serves as a beginning for further learning. Based on their individual strengths and leadership roles, the team members share with one another what has resonated for them from their experience as a committee working with Julia, and what areas they'll continue to explore. (*pp. 229-238*)

APPENDIX B

Foundation in Theory

The ideas presented in this book have made me a better leader, and contribute to my ability to support the growth of other leaders. They come from extensive reading and study, years of experience, and a variety of training. However, there is a foundation for my thinking that is a body of research and theory in Gestalt organizational development and leadership.

For those with no Gestalt familiarity the word comes from German and essentially means "whole." We use it in English to indicate the fullness of something as more than the sum of its parts. Gestalt as a theory has its roots in perceptual science – how we perceive and understand what we see – with old conclusions now being validated by new neuroscience research. Those basic principles were put to use in fields as varied as psychotherapy and graphic design.

This appendix explains the various Gestalt organizational and leadership concepts to which I refer in the book. I acknowledge that the interpretation I present is fully my own and you may find more academic explanations elsewhere. My interest in theory is in its application to the real world.

I attribute my core understanding of these concepts to Gestalt International Study Center founders Dr. Sonia March Nevis and the late Dr. Edwin Nevis and their lifelong work developing Gestalt theory, along with other senior GISC faculty including Joseph Melnick, Penny Bachman, and Joseph Zinker, all of whom I had the pleasure to study with. It was my greatest learning experience to be CEO at this Center for four years, working closely with Sonia and Ed, and I continue to be honored to serve on the faculty of GISC.

Awareness

You can't lead if you don't know who you are or where you're going, so at the core of leadership is your ability to see all that is going on in your environment (including yourself) and make some meaning from it. Then you need the skills to inspire others to be willing and able to follow.

Awareness comes first because new skills are useless if you aren't aware of what's going on in your environment, in yourself and those around you.

You can train yourself to increase your capacity to notice more so that your awareness becomes more sophisticated and discriminating, just like you can increase your ability to discern differences in wine, beer or chocolate.

Try an easy exercise. Start by writing down everything you are aware of right now. Everything. What's going on inside you, what's going on with others around you, what's in your environment that you can see, touch, smell, feel, or hear. That's just global awareness – being present to what is around you.

Then look over your list to notice how some of your statements are judgments. (The color of this room is ugly.) Some of your statements are just data. (This paint is chipping.) Notice how some are external—the room is square, and some are internal—I'm hungry.

If you do the exercise again, you'll see things you missed the first time around. Go deeper into detail, and larger into broader observations. You could do this exercise in your head first thing when you arrive at your office, increasing awareness about the people you'll meet or the challenges you'll face. Quickly you will discover that you are taking in far more subtleties and detail.

Paying attention means seeing with as much clarity as possible, including seeing those filters through which you interpret the world and which determine what you tend to see and what you tend to miss. Differences in culture, generations, training, family background, gender, etc. are all filters that determine what you notice and respond to.

Context also determines how we filter information. Since it is physically impossible to pay active attention to all the stimuli around us, our brains are constantly choosing what's important and what's not important. When my son was in an African game park doing research and sleeping in a tent, he paid careful attention when he heard grasses rustling outside. I'm unlikely to notice grasses rustling outside the window of my office when I'm preparing a budget.

Unfortunately, too many leaders allow their filters to blind them to important clues in their organization or in their marketplace. That's how Sony lost out to Apple and iTunes in the revolution of music distribution.

My colleague and friend, CEO John Wipfler, JD, MBA said it well. "In any one moment you are bombarded with multiple data points. Our own awareness is a filter for what we allow in and what we do with it. The more cleanly I take in information (without adding my biases) the more I open myself to my environment."

Increasing what you notice, whether it is happening inside you (internal) or happening outside you in the environment or within another person (external) is a key leadership skill. Using that knowledge to make more informed choices allows you to carry out the tasks of leadership effectively: developing a vision, executing on the vision, developing people, holding people accountable, achieving results.

Presence: Presence is how you impact and influence others. The higher you go in the organization, the more your presence is scrutinized and interpreted. Presence is composed of your personal style (appearance, body language, pace, energy level, etc.) as well as assumptions about yourself and others (values, intelligence, power, competence, wealth, etc.) Managing your presence intentionally is a key leadership behavior. Self awareness is the beginning of self management. Self-management is key to managing others.

You need to know how you want others to see you versus how they really do see you (your intention versus your impact). If you get too focused on results, you may forget to notice how you are impacting your people. You may intend to be collaborative and come across as indecisive. You could intend to be strong and come across as arrogant. You may think you're being helpful and instead are seen as controlling. Presence requires looking inward and looking out, being willing to ask for and accept feedback, and the discipline to practice new behaviors.

Optimistic Stance: When you pay attention, look for something to appreciate. It's not just the process of 'not judging,' it's a step beyond. Call it optimism at work—assuming that people and systems of people are doing the best they can, given the circumstances. That doesn't mean that what they do is good enough for the situation, it just means if they could do better they would. So what circumstances need to change to help them do better? It's a foundational assumption. When you notice a behavior in someone that isn't what you want, explore what works about it—how is it serving you or others? Let's say the front desk person at the hotel isn't keeping the coffee urn filled. If I look from an optimistic stance maybe I discover that the coffee maker is too far away and they don't want to leave the desk unattended, instead of assuming they are just slacking off and yelling at them. So I solve the problem by moving the coffee maker. Or maybe an employee stayed home today after an argument with someone yesterday. Looking from an optimistic stance I wonder how that served them and I find out that they didn't know how to face the person without blowing up so they managed their anger by staying away. I can appreciate their goal and help them find a way to learn to more effectively manage their anger in the moment. Looking from a stance of optimism allows you to see possibilities and find a base on which to make things better.

Contact: We can come together without really seeing each other or connecting, but when we stay aware and present, good contact is possible. This is true of our relationship to each other and to our environment. I can look out a window and be lost in thought and never notice the sunset, or drink in the colors and changing light. I can be introduced to you while seeing an important customer entering the room, and totally miss your name and who you are, or I can look you in the eyes, shake your hand and learn that you went to my high school. Leaders who learn to make good contact are more successful. Becoming more present and heightening your awareness of others leads to creating good contact, whether in conversation or in meetings. Leaders should also explore the contact that occurs between teams or divisions, and the quality of contact their organization makes with its public – customers and other stakeholders. In meetings, you can create the opportunity for better contact through framing the agenda or purpose – including knowing what action or outcome you want from participants, and how you want to allot the time available. You can teach your team a few tools for effective interactions: asking questions, taking your share of time, and refocusing your lens – the process of paying attention to what is going on inside you and what is going on in the other person or in the group. Though simple, they provide a foundation for creating better contact regardless of how difficult the content to be discussed.

Co-creation: The work we do with others and the interactions between us are always co-created. Think of painting a strip of juicy wet blue paint and a strip of juicy wet yellow paint right next to it on a wall. Where they touch you're going to get a strip of green – each color changes. The same happens when we bring our expectations and experiences and assumptions into contact with someone else. We are different with different people – outcomes are different. For example, if you are meeting with someone you expect to be difficult, you may find yourself more defensive or perhaps aggressive, which may intensify the other person's reaction. Attending to the assumptions you bring and the part you play in any interaction will heighten your ability to make choices and to have the impact you intend.

Cycle of Experience: The way we interact with and learn from our environment follows a natural cycle. Understanding its stages helps you to understand how to proceed through successfully, and how to help others. The cycle starts with encountering something new—a first awareness. Let's say you become annoyed because your car is in the shop again. It proceeds to a fuller engagement and exploration of that new idea, for example, counting back and realizing the car is six years old and you start to talk about maybe needing a new car. The next stage is one of examining and planning—data gathering and organizing. In the car example, you might read car magazines, visit dealers, or search online sites for information. At some point you become ready to move into action, actually choosing the model and making the purchase and driving the new car home. The final step of the cycle is evaluation and assimilation. You have learned all the car features, come to terms with what you like and what you don't like, and pretty soon you stop noticing that new car smell. The stages of the cycle give you a guide as to your progress, and a tool when you get stuck. At its simplest form, think about good beginnings, middles and endings. I won't want to follow you into action if I don't even see we have a problem. It's relevant from micro to macro. To build followership, leaders need this critical skill of being able to bring others successfully through the cycle—in conversations, meetings, change initiatives, and even creating brand awareness in their customers.

Multiple Realities: As you become more aware of the filters of experience and culture through which you see and interpret the world, you start to recognize and accept that others will be looking through different filters, leading them to a different interpretation of the same experience. It's as if you both look at the same sunset but your sunglasses are tinted red and their glasses are tinted blue. What you see and don't see will be different, but each of you will assume that what you see is "reality." We also see different realities based on where we stand. You see one side of a beach ball and it's yellow. I stand on the other side and it's blue. We might both work in the same company but if I work in sales and you work in engineering, we'll have entirely different realities. That's where conflict can occur. These "multiple realities" or different interpretations and visions of the same data or the same experience occur throughout our day, throughout our life. In the workplace, they become trickier to recognize because people tend to see work information, numerical data, financial performance, sales figures, etc., as "fact" and forget that we will each interpret such data based on our own filters. Think of that old story of the two salesmen who go to a rural village where everyone is barefoot. One sends a message to the home office saying "no market for shoes, no one wears them here." The other sends a message saying "great market for shoes, everyone needs them here." Same data, different conclusion. It is crucial for a leader to get curious about the other realities that are present in a conversation or a meeting or throughout their organization. Getting curious about what others see also helps them get more interested in what you might see, giving you both access to more information, greater flexibility, and the possibility of finding new solutions and achieving more buy-in.

Balancing Strategic and Intimate Behavior: Successful interactions, whether at work or in our personal lives, are always some combination of behavior that helps to connect us as human beings (intimate) and behavior that helps us get things done (strategic). When I see interactions that aren't working, it is frequently because the balance of strategic and intimate isn't appropriate. I've seen salespeople who build great relationships with their clients but never sell them a house (all intimate/not enough strategic interactions). I've experienced salespeople who try to sell me their product without building any relationship (all strategic/not enough intimate interactions). Or employers that love their people (intimate) but don't hold them accountable (strategic). Intimate behaviors build trust and help us become more interested in joining with the other to achieve something. Strategic behaviors help to define goals and accomplish them. Some situations require more strategic behaviors; sometimes more intimate behaviors are necessary. We tend to default more toward one or the other. We benefit by being aware of our default and expanding our range so we become skilled at providing the appropriate and necessary balance.

Polarities: Think of polarities as opposite ends of the same force, like the North and South poles. Understanding and using the concept of polarities in leadership starts with the recognition that all behavior falls somewhere on a continuum of one extreme to another. Someone can behave all the way from generous to stingy, or from active to passive. We tend to develop behavioral preferences or default styles toward one end or the other of a given continuum. With some behaviors we have a very narrow range, with others it may be wider. I can be quite bold and direct, or be subtle and gentle depending on what I think is appropriate or necessary. However, my pace of activity is far more likely to be rapid than slow. I have a broader range in the first example than the second. Increasing awareness of our default and experimenting with expanding our range on each continuum gives us more flexibility to respond and consequently more choice. If you tend to rely on being extremely organized, you may experience more success if you can *also* learn how to be spontaneous or flexible so you have a choice in situations that require it. No behavior is, in and of itself, either good or bad; its value is in its appropriateness. Ideally you want to be able to access the full range of the polarity, both in yourself and others, to give you the greatest flexibility.

Resistance: The first step to working with resistance is learning to appreciate that what you may label resistance is just a sign of differences based on our variety of experiences, needs, knowledge and perspective. Resistance (when it is the process of slowing or stopping movement) may be a natural protective mechanism for individuals and organizations. Just as you wouldn't want to drive a car that didn't have brakes, or have other cars approach you that didn't have brakes, we can appreciate the value of resistance in a change process. Those "resistors" may be protecting themselves from perceived fearful consequences, or they could be protecting the organization. They may, in fact, have more information about what is being changed than those who are initiating it. I think of an intersection of several roads near my house that was redesigned by safety experts because the construction crews demanded a change. One corner was so tight they couldn't even get their trucks around the turn. Thankfully, they were "resistant" to the design. Appreciating resistance allows us to get curious about it, and interested in what there is to learn, rather than evoking our own resistance to what we label resistance in others, and creating conflict. Getting curious leads us to see how resistance can take different forms (passive, active, underground, etc.) and can occur for different reasons—lack of understanding and information, not seeing the value, or mistrusting the person or the organization.

Paradox of Change: Ultimately we change by being accepting or acknowledging where we are. Change does not occur when we focus all our attention on what we are not. For example, if I talk about losing weight but I never own that I'm ten pounds more than is healthy for me, I have little likelihood of success. If I acknowledge what is actually going on I have more choice about whether to change my pattern. Similarly, an organization that is underperforming benchmarked against peers will only start to look for ways to improve if that fact is first acknowledged and the current contributors to performance are examined.

Figure and Ground: While I don't use these terms in the book, I reference this idea of looking across the information in our environment and making sense of all the data. Think of those old Magic Eye images which look like abstract art until we stop trying to see something and just let a picture emerge out of the background – that's figure and ground. The vast amount of data available to any leader is the ground. Some patterns or figures will emerge based on what we're looking for, and some patterns emerge because of our default perspective. If we, as individuals, teams, and organizations, allow ourselves more time to explore the ground, heightening our awareness of our environment, we have a better chance to create a successful understanding and response.

Level of System: Just as we envision the human body as a whole, and also a series of systems of varying size and complexity (the cell, the blood, the circulatory or respiratory systems), so too can we understand our human and organizational interactions. I can have an internal dialogue, I can talk with you alone, I can meet with my senior team, I can have a company wide meeting, I can address the shareholders, I can Tweet with the world. Each entity is a system alone and connects to others to create a larger system. Are my poor sales the result of an ineffective sales manager, poor communication between sales and manufacturing, a new competitor, a change in customer usage, or an economic downturn? As leaders we need to understand where we are working in the system, especially when leading change and problem solving.

Support: Getting support, especially when stuck, is at the heart of this book. Leaders tend to be independent, relying on themselves, used to having to appear invulnerable. Maybe it's the meeting for which they do it all: set the agenda, facilitate, manage time, resolve conflict, and initiate follow up. Sometimes it's the weight of difficult conflicts that they carry alone. They sit in the organizational system without peers and deal with issues of high sensitivity and confidentiality. They also may lack opportunities for honest feedback. How does anyone learn or grow under those circumstances? Whether getting support means going outside the organization, or finding it within, don't always go it alone, and if you find yourself facing the same challenge over and over again, it's time to get help.

~~~~~~~~~~~~~~

Nancy Hardaway is passionate about increasing success and satisfaction for leaders and organizations. This book is an introduction, but all leaders should find a source of support outside of themselves. You can find more information about the concepts contained in this book, Nancy's work, and her company, Listening 2 Leaders, on her website. She is an entertaining and compelling speaker and welcomes inquiries to speak to your company or organization about *The Awareness Paradigm,* or to support your leadership development. Inquire at Info@Listening2Leaders.com or visit her website at Listening2Leaders.com.

CPSIA information can be obtained at www.ICGtesting.com
Printed in the USA
BVOW03s1123230813

329304BV00005B/17/P